THE BRITISH LIBRARY

writers' lives

Samuel Taylor Coleridge

In a vision once I saw:
It was an Abyssinian Maid,
And on her Dulcimer she play'd
Singing of Mount Amara.
Could I revive within me
Her Symphony & Song,
To such a deep Delight 'twould win me,
That with Music loud and long
I would build that Dome in Air,
That sunny Dome! those caves of Ice!
And all, who heard, should see them there,
And all should cry, Beware! Beware!
His flashing Eyes! his floating Hair!
Weave a circle round him thrice,
And close your Eyes in holy Dread:
For He on Honey-dew hath fed
And drank the Milk of Paradise.————

This fragment with a good deal more, not
recoverable, composed, in a sort of Reverie brought
on by two grains of Opium, taken to check a
dysentery, at a Farm House between Porlock &
Linton, a quarter of a mile from Culbone Church,
in the fall of the year, 1797.————

S. T. Coleridge

THE BRITISH LIBRARY
writers' lives

Samuel Taylor Coleridge

SEAMUS PERRY

THE BRITISH LIBRARY

 # Contents

7   **THE YOUNGEST SON 1772–1794**

17   **THE PANTISOCRAT 1794–1797**

36   **WORDSWORTH 1797–1799**

56   **THE LAKES 1799–1804**

78   **MALTA 1804–1806**

85   **LONDON AND THE LAKES 1806–1810**

97   **MAN OF LETTERS 1810–1816**

109   **SAGE OF HIGHGATE 1816–1834**

122   **CHRONOLOGY**

124   **FURTHER READING**

126   **INDEX**

Samuel Taylor Coleridge

Places in England where
Samuel Taylor Coleridge
lived, travelled and
wrote.

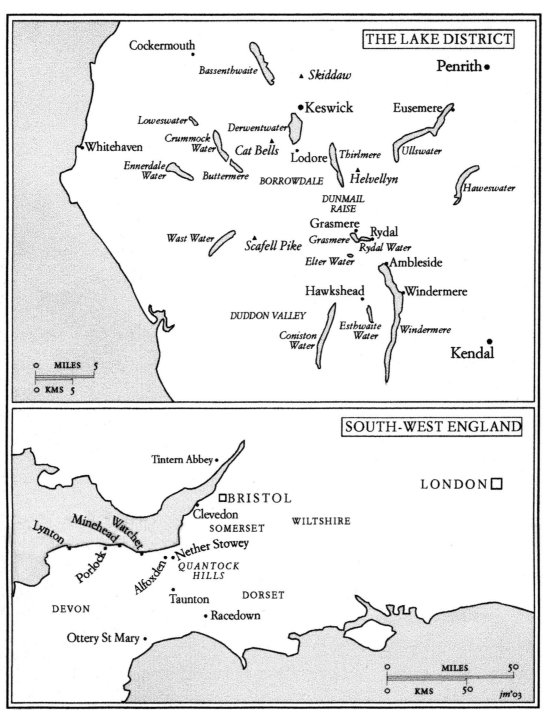

The Youngest Son 1772–1794

Samuel Taylor Coleridge always understood his birthday to be 20 October – a date he came to dread as it recurred to remind him of things undone. Oddly enough, he had the date wrong: in fact he was born on 21 October, 1772. As a young radical, he liked to boast his 'veins uncontaminated with one drop of Gentility', which was true: his father, the Reverend John Coleridge, was the son of a Devon draper. John was set up as a schoolmaster; he married and had children. At the late age of twenty-eight, he was admitted as a student to Sidney Sussex College, Cambridge, where he quickly distinguished himself; but a fellowship (a senior membership of the college) was out of the question because he was married, and he returned to Devon to become a headmaster. His first wife died, and in 1754 he remarried; his bride was Ann Bowdon, daughter of a family of Exmoor farmers.

Coleridge would recall his father as a saintly and unworldly figure, the subject of funny stories: 'in learning, good-heartedness, absentness of mind, & excessive ignorance of the world, he was a perfect *Parson Adams*', the simple and kindly curate from Henry Fielding's novel *Joseph Andrews*. But in truth John Coleridge was highly gifted and clearly not without ambition, and in 1760 he was appointed headmaster of the King's Grammar School and vicar of the handsome church of St Mary's in the town of Ottery in east Devon – an eminent station after so humble a beginning. He published a number of books, including *A Miscellaneous Dissertation Arising from the 17th and 18th Chapters of the Book of Judges*, which, as Coleridge's friend and biographer James Gillman said, 'commences ... with a well written preface on the Bible,

and ends with an advertisement of his school, and his method of teaching Latin'. His son's works would sometimes take only marginally less peculiar forms.

John and Ann Coleridge had nine sons and one daughter. (John had four, much older, daughters from his first marriage, who play no part in our story.) Samuel was the youngest. He was christened after one of his godfathers, so saddling him with a name he came to loathe, 'the wabble it makes, & staggering between a diss- & a tri-syllable … altogether it is perhaps the worst combination, of which vowels & consonants are susceptible'. In darker moments, his name seemed to symbolise the wobbliness of will for which Coleridge often chastised himself: he much preferred to be known by his more resolute-sounding initials, 'STC'.

The Coleridge children were industrious and accomplished. The eldest son John was in India, working for the East India Company; another, James, was to pursue a distinguished career in the army before returning to Ottery St Mary where he lived in the Chantry House. Others went to Oxford and became clergymen and teachers, including George, 'a man of reflective mind & elegant Genius', to whom Coleridge was closest; one, Luke, trained as a doctor in London, and died in his twenties; the single sister, Anne, who was much loved, died of consumption at twenty-one. Young Samuel was the favourite: 'My father was very fond of me, and I was my mother's darling – in consequence, I was very miserable'. Relations with Francis Sydercombe, the sibling nearest him in age, seem to have been especially rivalrous. Frank, known to the family as 'the handsome Coleridge', was boisterous and unstudious, and so Samuel's opposite: he regarded his younger brother, STC recalled, 'with a strange mixture of admiration & contempt'. One confrontation over a piece of cheese provoked the seven-year-old Samuel to run at his brother with a knife; fearing his mother's rebuke, he fled the house and spent the night freezing in the open air by the River Otter, only to be discovered the next morning. The memory of 'that night, I slept out at Ottery' returned to Coleridge years later, when he recorded it in his notebook, and it reappears in the lines of 'Dejection: An Ode' that describe 'a little child | Upon a lonesome wild, | Not far from home, but she hath lost her way'. He rarely lost a sense of abandonment.

'I became a *dreamer*', Coleridge later said of his childhood, 'and acquired an indisposition to all bodily activity' – throughout his life he would have a reputation for being (as he put it) 'reverie-ish & streamy'. He joined his father's school at six – 'and soon outstripped all of my age'. He was precociously bookish, and especially taken by the *Arabian Nights*, 'one tale of which', he remembered, 'made so deep an impression on me (I read it in the evening while my mother was mending stockings) that I was haunted by spectres, whenever I was in the dark'. When his father discovered the effect of the tales he had the books burned; but, in later life, Coleridge would claim that his 'early reading of Faery Tales, & Genii' had shaped his growing mind in an entirely beneficial way for thanks to it, he maintained, 'my mind had been habituated *to the Vast* – & I never regarded *my senses* in any way as the criteria of my belief'. His senses were often astonishingly acute, but much of the adult Coleridge's philosophy would build upon the principle that the ideas of the mind are nobler and more profound than the merely sensory perceptions of the body.

In the autumn of 1781, John Coleridge travelled with Frank to Plymouth, where Frank was to set sail for a military career in India. (He was to die there, a terrible end, killing himself after fighting in the battle for Seringapatam in 1792, part

The Hall of 'The Blue Coat School' by T. Rowlandson and C.A. Pugin (c.1810). Two Grecians (the school's top scholars) are declaiming in the centre of the hall. Coleridge joined Christ's Hospital – with its distinctive blue coat uniform – in 1782 and was made a Grecian in 1788.

The British Museum 1902–12–11–1

of a long series of wars that led to the establishment of English rule in Mysore.) On John Coleridge's return home on 4 October, he repeated to his wife a strange dream of the night before about Death. He went to bed in good spirits and within minutes he was dead. Ann's screams awoke Samuel, and he later remembered his response: 'I said, "Papa is dead" … How I came to think of his Death, I cannot tell; but so it was'. Samuel continued as a pupil at the Grammar School for a time, but in the spring of 1782 an influential former pupil of his late father put the boy's name forward for Christ's Hospital, the renowned charity school, then in Newgate Street, London. He was accepted for the autumn term and moved to the city, spending the weeks before his admission lodging with Ann Coleridge's brother, Bowdon, a kindly man, a tobacconist and drinker: 'My Uncle was very proud of me, & used to carry me from Coffee-house to Coffee-house, and Tavern to Tavern, where I drank, & talked & disputed, as if I had been a man … Nothing was more common than for a large party to exclaim in my hearing, that I *was a prodigy*'. In July, he 'donned the *Blue* coat & yellow Stockings', the school's distinctive uniform, and was sent to Christ's Hospital preparatory school in Hertford, a little outside the capital, where he spent six happy and well-fed weeks.

In September, it was time to return to London to attend the main school, where the regime was much harsher: 'O! what a change!', Coleridge later recalled, 'Depressed, moping, friendless, poor orphan, half-starved'. In fact, he was not quite friendless: he still saw the Bowdons; he was close to his brother Luke, who was studying at the London Hospital, and he regularly wrote to George – whom he now thought of as 'father, brother, and every thing to me'. But his recollections of that time are almost uniformly forlorn – those of an isolated orphan with 'scarce any connections in London'. These are the imprisoned days portrayed later in 1802 in the verse 'Letter to Sara Hutchinson', 'cloister'd in a city School | The Sky was all, I knew, of Beautiful', and also in 'Frost at Midnight', where Coleridge sadly contrasts his own deprived upbringing with the wandering natural freedom he imagines for his own son: 'I was reared | In the great city, pent 'mid cloisters dim, | And saw nought lovely but the sky and stars'.

Samuel was prodigious – 'there was something awful about him', a contemporary recalled, 'for all his equals in age and rank quailed before him'. He still read obsessively: 'My whole being was, with eyes closed to every object of present sense, to crumple myself up in a sunny corner, and read, read, read'. He had a subscription to a circulating library, earned (as he later told the story) in odd circumstances. In a daydream one day, imagining himself to be the classical hero Leander swimming the Hellespont, the young Coleridge inadvertently swung his hand into the pocket of a passer-by, who reasonably took him for a thief – but as soon as Coleridge offered his tearful explanation, the gentleman was so charmed that, instead of reproving the child, he bought him a library ticket. The tale is typical of many to come, with Coleridge charming his way by the strange power of his speech. Among the boys at Christ's Hospital was Charles Lamb, subsequently famous for his delightfully sad and funny *Essays of Elia*, in which he warmly recalled Coleridge's legendary gifts. In the essay 'Christ's Hospital Five and Thirty Years Ago', Lamb remembers casual passers-by, drawn into the school cloisters and 'intranced with admiration' at the extraordinary conversation of 'the *inspired charity-boy*'.

Charles Lamb, drawn by Robert Hancock (1798). Lamb was Coleridge's contemporary at Christ's Hospital, and later one of his closest friends. Coleridge appears as a schoolboy prodigy in Lamb's essay 'Christ's Hospital Five and Thirty Years Ago'.

The Wordsworth Trust

Coleridge came to the attention of the school authorities when an older boy discovered him reading Virgil for pleasure and told the headmaster. Thus it was that Coleridge came to enjoy the ambiguous advantage of the Reverend James Bowyer's full attention. Bowyer (or Boyer), master of the upper grammar school, swiftly decided that Coleridge was to become a 'Grecian'. (The Grecians were the school's academic elite, destined for Oxford or Cambridge.) In *Biographia Literaria*, his great prose work, Coleridge describes Bowyer as 'a very sensible, though at the same time, a very severe master', which is very mild: whatever his virtues, Bowyer was a violent monster who regarded flogging as vocation. Coleridge did not escape, as his first biographer James Gillman recorded: 'he was so ordinary a looking boy, with his black head, that Bowyer generally gave him at the end of a flogging an extra cut; "for," said he, " you are such an ugly fellow!" '. In *Biographia* Coleridge attributes to Bowyer an important critical truth, that 'Poetry, even that of the loftiest, and, seemingly, that of the wildest odes, had a logic of its own, as severe as that of science'. That puts Bowyer in a kindly light, but according to the poet and essayist Leigh Hunt, another Christ's Hospital boy, Coleridge had nightmares about his old master all his life.

The unhappiness of school was soothed by Coleridge's growing intimacy with the family of Tom Evans, a fellow pupil. Coleridge came to regard his friendship with the Evanses as a kind of salvation, rescuing him from his bookish self-absorption. (He would often hopefully invest his personal relationships with a power to redeem him from his own inadequacies, a burden of expectation which inevitably put his friendships under great strain.) Coleridge would stay in touch with the Evanses over the following years, writing them vivacious and flirty letters from university, and he grew especially preoccupied with the thought of the eldest daughter, Mary: 'I loved her … almost to madness', he later said.

Two events of 1789 would affect the sixteen-year-old Coleridge lastingly. In July, a mob in Paris stormed the Bastille, a grim fortress which had come to represent the oppression and despotism of the French King. The fall of the Bastille precipitated revolution, and ultimately the institution of a republic: the protracted upheaval was the central political event for Coleridge's generation. Coleridge wrote an exuberant poem about it: 'Yes! Liberty the soul of Life shall reign, | Shall throb in every pulse, shall flow thro' every vein!' Such excitement was far from odd: 'I trust there are many

of my Readers of the same age with myself', he later wrote in his periodical *The Friend*, 'who will throw themselves back into the state of thought and feeling in which they were when France was reported to have solemnized her first sacrifice of error and prejudice on the bloodless altar of Freedom, by an oath of peace and good-will to all mankind'. His attitude toward the Revolution in France changed a good deal as he grew older, but his rhetoric here momentarily recaptures an earlier exuberance.

The other event effected a personal revolution: Coleridge acquired a copy of a new book, *Sonnets, Written Chiefly in Picturesque Spots* by the clergyman-poet William Lisle Bowles, by which he was (as he recalled in *Biographia*) 'delighted and inspired'. After the intense abstraction of his intellectual life, he felt that the sonnets had renewed his 'fancy, and the love of nature, and the sense of beauty in forms and sounds'. Bowles appears a very minor writer now, but his interweaving of inward feeling and outward description struck Coleridge deeply, and provided a kind of model. He copied out the poems and distributed them to friends, and later produced a printed sheet of sonnets for which he wrote a preface in which he praised their 'sweet and indissoluble union between the intellectual and the material world'. ('Intellectual' at this period means something like 'mental' or 'spiritual'.) The 'union' he describes affords an early glimpse of a central theme in Coleridge's literary thinking: the belief that 'A Poet's *Heart & Intellect* should be *combined*, *intimately* combined & *unified*, with the great appearances in Nature', or that, as he put it elsewhere, 'In every work of art there is a reconcilement of the external with the internal'. Bowles was a slight talent to bear such critical weight, but Coleridge would shortly find a more substantial exemplification of the genius he was looking for, in Wordsworth.

Coleridge left school in September 1791, marking the occasion with a regretful sonnet of his own: 'Farewell parental scenes!' He was a great success: Senior Grecian, with a place at Jesus College, Cambridge. Once he arrived at the university, his college promptly awarded him a scholarship and, the following year, he won the prestigious Browne gold medal for an ode in Greek – altogether, a most brilliant beginning. In his second year he entered the competition for a University scholarship. The person who won it, Samuel Butler, later headmaster of Shrewsbury School, recalled Coleridge working very hard for the exam, and Coleridge himself may have been exaggerating when he subsequently wailed to George, 'for the whole six weeks, that preceded the examination, I was almost constantly intoxicated! My Brother, you shudder as you read'. But whatever the truth about that, his failure in the competition was a real set back – because, at that time, there was no Classics Tripos (the Cambridge University examination), the scholarship had been one of the few ways to distinguish himself.

But perhaps thoughts of an academic future were fading anyway. Classical scholarship was becoming overshadowed by current affairs, and Greek authors supplanted by the flurry of pamphlets and political essays (such as those by the great statesman Edmund Burke) that had appeared following the Revolution in France. A student contemporary later recalled life in Coleridge's set:

> *What evenings have I spent in those rooms! What little suppers, or* sizings, *as they were called, have I enjoyed; when Æschylus, and Plato, and Thucydides were pushed aside, with a pile of lexicons, &c. to discuss the pamplets of the day. Ever and anon, a pamphlet issued from the pen of Burke. There was no need of having the book before us. Coleridge had read it in the morning, and in the evening he would repeat whole pages verbatim. Frend's trial was then in progress.*

William Frend was a Fellow of Jesus College, and a figure of some controversy in the university. George Coleridge, an Anglican minister, had already fretted about his brother's proximity to so notorious a figure, and Coleridge's joshing reply cannot have been very reassuring: 'Mr Frend's company is by no means invidious ... I have yet *prudence* enough to *respect* that *gluttony of Faith* waggishly yclept Orthodoxy'. (The bantering archaism of 'waggishly yclept' – meaning 'mischievously named' – implies Coleridge's teasing high spirits.) Frend was not religiously orthodox – he was a Unitarian: that is to say, he denied the Holy Trinity of Father, Son and Holy Spirit in which Anglicans (and other Christians) believe, holding instead that Jesus was a mortal man – an exemplarily good man, but not divine, the son of Joseph, and not the son of God. Politically, too, Frend was contentious, making positive noises about revolutionary France, with whom Britain was by now at war. In neither his theology nor his politics was Frend exactly outlandish – much liberal opinion of the time was similarly non-conformist in religion and politically sympathetic toward the ambitions of the French revolutionaries – but the University of Cambridge was not a stronghold of liberal opinion. Things came to a head in May 1793, when the university authorities put Frend on trial for publishing a pamphlet called *Peace and Union*, deemed to defame the Anglican church. A radicalised generation of undergraduates, Coleridge prominent among them, vociferously supported the accused. An associate later remembered him joining a group writing 'Frend for Ever' in chalk on walls throughout the town.

Jesus College, Cambridge, where Coleridge studied from 1791 to 1794.

The British Library, 127 i.11 Vol.2

At this point Coleridge's glittering undergraduate career began to fall apart. He was badly in debt, and he turned to his brothers for help, writing contritely of his errors to George: 'I trust, the Memory of them will operate to future consistency of Conduct'. But consistency of conduct was never much of a Coleridgean virtue, and the money was soon gone again. He made his way to London where, wandering forlornly, he bought a ticket in the Irish Lottery, and wrote a poem of jokey but bleak feelings, 'To Fortune', which he sent off to the *Morning Chronicle*: 'O haste with fost'ring hand to rear | One Flower of Hope!' He fleetingly reappeared in Cambridge again in early November, but he was soon back in London, where, as he later recalled, he glumly walked the streets and gave his last coins to beggars. Then, seeing a recruitment poster, he impulsively enlisted in the 15th Light Dragoons, and a couple of days later he was sworn in at Reading, in Berkshire, under the improbable pseudonym 'Silas Tomkyn Comberbache'.

Later in life Coleridge made a comic turn of his brief and unsuccessful military career, making fun of his incompetence as 'a very indocile Equestrian'. But the experience was really not so droll: he was posted to nurse a fellow dragoon who had contracted smallpox, and the references he makes at the time to 'almost total want of Sleep, the putrid smell and the fatiguing Struggles with my poor Comrade during his delirium' suggest a wretched time. His identity was eventually discovered, or so the story was later told, when his doodles written on the wall in Latin were spotted by an officer. News reached Coleridge's brothers, who managed to buy him out, and he was discharged 'Insane' on 10 April 1794. Back in Cambridge, the Fellows of his college issued him with a formal reprimand. He resolved to work hard, preparing, he told George, 'for all the Prizes'; but his academic life was about to be interrupted again, this time irreparably.

The Pantisocrat 1794–1797

In June 1794, Coleridge set off from Cambridge with a friend, one Joseph Hucks, bound for a walking tour through North Wales. They stopped off on their way at Oxford, where Coleridge looked in on an old Christ's Hospital contemporary, who, in turn, introduced him to a charismatic undergraduate at Balliol College – Robert Southey. Southey had been expelled from school at Westminster for campaigning against corporal punishment, and he had continued to propagate ostentatiously progressive views at Oxford. He declared himself a republican, and zealously embraced the atheistic philosophy of William Godwin (subsequently the husband of Mary Wollstonecraft and father of Mary Shelley). Godwin's *Enquiry concerning Political Justice* (1793), was a favourite book among young radical intellectuals, with a thesis which was simple to grasp: all suffering and crime was due to social inequality, and removing that required the abolition of private property. Godwin's equitable Utopia appealed purely to human reason – and despite the manifest fallibility of human reason, he still managed to suggest that the transformation in affairs he prescribed was somehow excitingly imminent.

Throughout his life, Coleridge needily revered a succession of men whom he perceived to be stronger and more resolute than himself – Thomas Poole and William Wordsworth would each find themselves playing such a part in time, and for the moment the role was squarely filled by Southey. Coleridge was immediately taken with his new acquaintance – 'truly a man of *perpendicular Virtue*', as he was to say, 'a *down-right, upright Republican!*' His own radicalism, ignited by the Frend affair, was soon flaming energetically again. Coleridge and Hucks had intended to stay in Oxford for three or four days but ended staying three weeks, during which time Coleridge and Southey sketched out the scheme of a society in which all possessions would be held in common and (so it followed) all incentives to evil and unhappiness removed: 'The real source of inconstancy, depravity, & prostitution', Coleridge declared roundly, 'is *Property*, which mixes with & poisons every thing good – & is beyond doubt the Origin of all Evil'. Southey came at the idea from Godwinian principles; Coleridge, who always resisted Godwin's atheism, arrived at his spiritual

*Robert Southey, by
Peter Vandyke (1795).
Coleridge's meeting
with Southey, in the
summer of 1794, was
to change his life.
Southey was, he
reported, 'a man of
perpendicular Virtue',
with an 'undeviating
Simplicity and
Rectitude'.*

National Portrait Gallery

communism from a more idiosyncratically religious inspiration. He liked to cite the Biblical text, 'And all that believed were together, & had all things in common' (Acts II, 44) – a passage which, he provocatively explained, constituted 'almost the whole' of Christian doctrine. His exhilarating conversations with Southey were of more than merely theoretical interest. They rapidly decided that they would establish a real settlement 'on the banks of the Susquehannah' (in Pennsylvania), and quickly found some similarly idealistic recruits to the scheme, including George Burnet and Robert Lovell, both Balliol men. Coleridge confidently reported later that summer: 'the time of emigration we have fixed on next March'. He invented a name for their political scheme: 'Pantisocracy'.

Belatedly, he set off with Hucks for Gloucester, travelling on into Wales. At an inn at Llanfyllin, near Welshpool, Coleridge preached Pantisocracy (as he reported back to Southey) 'with so much success that two great huge Fellows, of Butcher like appearance, danced about the room in enthusiastic agitation'. At Bala, he pledged a toast to George Washington and nearly provoked a bar-room brawl. He and Hucks passed through Llangollen, 'a village most romantically situated', thought Coleridge, though the weather was oppressively hot, and they pressed on to Caernarfon and the Isle of Anglesey, before turning to home. As he travelled, he wrote exuberant letters back to Southey. 'I have positively done nothing', he told his new comrade, 'but dream of the System of no Property every step of the Way since I left you … Heigho! –'

Coleridge made for Bristol, where Southey was now living. During the Welsh tour, the revolutionary leader Robespierre had been executed in France and, with a thought of raising money to fund their emigration, the Pantisocrats co-authored a timely play, *The Fall of Robespierre*, which was published in September. They went walking in the Quantock Hills in nearby Somerset, and in the little village of Nether Stowey they made the acquaintance of Thomas Poole, an affluent tanner with democratic sympathies. Poole was to become one of Coleridge's most important friends and supporters, 'the man in whom *first* and in whom alone, I had felt an *anchor*!' as Coleridge emotionally told him five years later. Poole was greatly struck by both the young men, but by Coleridge especially, and he listened to their political ideas with sceptical indulgence: 'Could they realise them', he wrote to a friend, 'they

Following pages:

Llangollen, North Wales, *by J.M.W. Turner (1794) – the landscape that Coleridge and Hucks passed through on their tour in the summer of 1794.*

Whitworth Art Gallery, Manchester

would, indeed, realise the age of reason'. Moved by a spirit of mischief, presumably, Poole introduced them to his ultra-respectable cousin John, whose response was predictably less favourable: 'Each of them was shamefully hot with Democratic rage as regards politics, and both Infidel as to religion', fumed John Poole in his diary, 'I was extremely indignant'.

Thomas Poole, an engraving from Mrs Henry Stanford's Thomas Poole and his Friends *(1888). Poole was one of Coleridge's most loyal and supportive friends.*

The British Library, 10827 bbb18

Back in Bristol, the democratic rage grew hotter. Inextricably linked with the scheme to emigrate, Coleridge now became intimate with the Fricker family, a widow and five daughters. Robert Lovell was already married to Mary Fricker, and Southey was intending to marry her sister Edith; and, mostly it seems for reasons of symmetry, Coleridge became engaged to Sarah, the eldest daughter, whose name (for some unknown reason) he chose to respell 'Sara'. Sara was clever and stylish and quick-witted, and what she made of the sudden prospect of marriage to Coleridge is hard to imagine. Years later, she recalled him as she first saw him, 'plain, but eloquent and clever', 'brown as a berry' from his Welsh tour, and badly in need of a haircut – to an elegant young woman like herself, 'a dreadful figure'. Southey, always a much more dapper figure, kindly reassured her, 'he is a diamond set in lead'.

The omens for the marriage were bad almost from the start. 'Yes – Southey – you are right', Coleridge declared to his putative brother-in-law in September, 'Even Love is the creature of strong Motive – I certainly love her'. In fact, he soon realised he had misconstrued his true feelings, distracted by the excitements of pantisocratic theory – 'having mistaken the ebullience of *schematism* for affection', as he put it to Southey. But things rapidly acquired an irresistible momentum as Coleridge whirled about London, Bath and Cambridge, evangelising about a new communal life by the Susquehannah. Mary Evans, his first love, heard of the scheme, and attempted to dissuade him from so reckless a course: 'There is an Eagerness in your Nature, which is ever hurrying you into the sad Extreme', which was true enough. Coleridge was still much in love with Mary, as he made clear: 'She WAS VERY lovely, Southey! We formed each other's minds – our ideas were blended'. But Southey was not listening, or did not recognise what he was hearing, and Coleridge felt unable to resist his perpendicular virtue: 'I am resolved – but wretched! – But Time shall do much'. He learnt at the end of the year that Mary was engaged to marry someone else and wrote her a sad note asking her to forget his letters.

Mary Evans may have been prompted to write by George, who, having rescued Coleridge from the army, must have thought his young brother saved from one disaster only to launch himself into another. When George made some anxious enquiries, Coleridge wrote reassuringly, seeking to defuse any rumours that he was 'a D[e]mocrat' and presenting himself instead as merely a faithful Christian – which was hardly ingenuous, since we have seen, Coleridge's religious beliefs were inextricable from his utopian politics. If poor George had been still hoping to see Samuel return to university he was soon disappointed, for in December, Coleridge finally quit Cambridge altogether and installed himself in London at the Salutation and Cat, a tavern in Newgate Street. During this period he forged one of his most lasting friendships, with Charles Lamb, his old schoolmate, who would long recall

NEW MORALITY;— or *The promis'd Installment of the High-Priest of the* THEOPHILANTHROPES, *with the Homage of Leviathan and his Suite.*

fondly the thought of 'that nice little smoky room at the Salutation … with all its associate train of pipes, tobacco, egg-hot, Welsh-rabbits, metaphysics, and poetry'.

Coleridge published a series of political sonnets in the *Morning Chronicle*, including an outspoken one on Prime Minister Pitt, whom he likened to Judas Iscariot. He also printed an effusion 'To a Young Ass', a poem of tender Pantisocratic feelings addressed to a subjugated donkey, which fraternally proclaimed, 'I hail thee BROTHER – spite of the fool's scorn!' And he certainly did earn a good deal of scorn: a few years later, in *The New Morality* (1798), James Gillray's marvellous caricature of the British radical movement, Coleridge appears with a handsome pair of ass's ears.

The lines to the young ass make Coleridge's fraternal feelings towards other creatures sound simply dotty, and he was at least partly sending himself up. But 'Religious Musings', a long philosophical poem which he began on Christmas Eve 1794, sets out the political and theological views which lie behind that sense of brotherhood in deadly earnest, couched in a fervent, knotty blank verse based on John Milton:

'Tis the sublime of man,

Our noontide Majesty, to know ourselves

Parts and proportions of one wond'rous whole:

This fraternises man, this constitutes

Our charities and bearings. But 'tis God

Diffused through all, that doth make all one whole ...

Opposite page:

New Morality *(1798),
James Gillray's satirical
masterpiece, pictures the
English radicals paying
homage before the altar
of revolution. Standing
either side of the
'Cornucopia of Ignorance',
Coleridge and Southey,
both with asses' ears,
declaim their poetry.
Behind them, Coleridge's
friends Charles Lamb and
Charles Lloyd, a frog and
a toad, read out their
blank verse. To their left,
John Thelwall, the great
radical orator and an
acquaintance of Coleridge,
can also be seen reciting.*

The British Library, PP3595

The sense is contorted, but it is worth unpicking, not only because Coleridge himself thought well of the poem for a time, but also because its doctrine lies behind many of his other, greater early poems. To paraphrase, then. The highest pinnacle of human experience ('the sublime of man, | Our noontide Majesty') is to apprehend your place in the encompassing oneness of God ('Parts and proportions of one wond'rous whole'); and the effect of this realisation is to make you feel yourself a member of the universal family of Creation – this makes you know yourself the brother ('This fraternises man') of your fellow creatures, to whom you now owe a duty of love and relationship ('this constitutes | Our charities and bearings'). It is a kind of spiritual ecology.

Coleridge's lines draw heavily on the works of Joseph Priestley, the leading Unitarian thinker of the period. George's fears had evidently been realised, and William Frend's Unitarianism had taken firm root. For mainstream Christians, like Anglican George, God enters the world in the incarnation of Christ, but, obviously, a Unitarian God could not be present in the world in that way. However, this did not mean that He was not present in the world at all – on the contrary, for Priestley and his followers, God is immanent within all nature, a ubiquitous, in-dwelling creativity, gathering all things into the unity of His pervasive life: ''tis God | Diffused through all, that doth make all one whole'. As Priestley had said of God, in a book called *Matter and Spirit* which Coleridge read, 'His power is the very *life and soul* of every thing that exists'. The idea was enormously appealing to Coleridge, who (had he known about him) would have agreed with the proclamation of his visionary contemporary William Blake: 'every thing that lives is holy'. Coleridge seriously entertained thoughts of entering the Unitarian ministry during the later 1790s, and he preached in several West Country chapels evidently to great effect. As a young man, the essayist William

Hazlitt heard him in the pulpit at Shrewsbury and never forgot it: 'Poetry and Philosophy had met together, Truth and Genius had embraced, under the eye and with the sanction of Religion'. Another listener remembered: 'he burst from the sermon, which he abruptly terminated, into a fervent address to the Deity', a prayer which 'impressed all present as the most sublime devotional exercise they had ever heard'.

But that was still to come. The last weeks of 1794 found Coleridge still snugly settled with Lamb in the bachelor life of the 'Salutation and Cat', and clearly reluctant to return to Bristol and Southey – and to Sara, who was now his intended. He had announced his imminent arrival several times without showing up, and finally, in January 1795, an exasperated Southey made the journey to London to reclaim his stray. Lamb missed Coleridge's company sadly – as, according to Lamb, did the landlord of the Salutation and Cat, who entreated Coleridge to stay and even 'offered him free quarters if he would only talk'.

Bristol was a centre of the radical movement because, as an Atlantic port, it was deeply involved with the slave trade, the focal point of much activism. Coleridge threw himself into the city's political life, giving three rousing addresses in February, intended 'to disseminate Truth' as well as to raise money to subsidise the American emigration. The first lecture was so fiery that he had to publish it to defuse rumours of its treasonableness. An older Coleridge's sadder and wiser recollections of his oratory suggest how his 'disposition to catch fire by the very rapidity of my own motion' might have carried him away:

> *Speaking in public at Bristol I adverted to a public Supper which had been given by Lord – I forget his name, in honor of a victory gained by the Austrians, & after a turbid Stream of wild Eloquence I said – 'This is a true Lord's Supper in the communion of Darkness! This is a Eucharist of Hell! A sacrament of Misery! – Over each morsel & each Drop of which the Spirit of some murdered Innocent cries aloud to God, This is* my Body! *& this is my Blood! –' – These words form alas! a faithful specimen of too many of my Declamations at that Time.*

His lectures were certainly provocative: 'Two or three uncouth and unbrained Automata have threatened my Life', Coleridge reported to a correspondent,

S. T. COLERIDGE,

Proposes to give in SIX LECTURES a COMPARATIVE VIEW of the

ENGLISH REBELLION under CHARLES the First,

AND THE

FRENCH REVOLUTION.

The SUBJECTS of the proposed LECTURES are,

I.

THE distinguishing Marks of the French and English Character with their probable Causes. The national Circumstances precursive to (1) the English Rebellion, (2) the French Revolution.

II.

The Liberty of the Press. Literature—its revolutionary Powers. Comparison of the English with the French political Writers at the time of the several Revolutions. MILTON. SYDNEY. HARRINGTON. BRISSOT. SEYEYES. MIRABEAU. THOMAS PAYNE.

III.

The fanaticism of the (1) English, and (2) French Revolutionists. English Sectaries. French Parties:—Feuillans, Girondists, Faction of Hebert, Jacobins, Moderants, Royalists.

IV.

1. Characters of Charles Ist and Louis the XVIth. 2. Of Louis the XIVth and the present Empress of Russia. 3. Lives and Characters of *Essex* and *Fayette.*

V.

OLIVER CROMWELL, and ROBESPIERRE.—CARDINAL MAZARINE, and WILLIAM PITT.—DUNDAS, and BARRERE.

VI.

On Revolution in general—its moral Causes, and probable effects on the revolutionary People, and surrounding Nations.

It is intended, that the Lectures should be given once a Week, on TUESDAY EVENINGS, at Eight o'Clock, at the ASSEMBLY COFFEE HOUSE, on the QUAY.—The first Lecture, on Tuesday, June 23, 1795. As the Author wishes to insure an Audience adequate to the Expences of the Room, he has prepared Subscription Tickets for the whole course, price SIX SHILLINGS, which may be had at the Lecture Room, and at Mr. REED's, Bookseller, Wine-Street.

BIGGS, PRINTER.

The Prospectus for a course of political lectures, announced by Coleridge in the summer of 1795 but probably never delivered.

The British Library, Add MS 35343 f.71v

sounding shaken that his robot-like antagonists 'were scarcely restrained from attacking the house in which the "damn'd Jacobine was jawing away"'. (It is no surprise that Coleridge's opponents thought of him as a 'Jacobine' or 'Jacobin': the *Jacobins* were the extreme political party in revolutionary France, and their name was used in English as a derogatory term for anyone who, like Coleridge, sympathised with the aims of political reform.)

Prudently, Coleridge abandoned his lectures; but, in May 1795 he returned undaunted to the platform with a series of six 'Lectures on Revealed Religion, Its Corruptions, and its Political Views'. Like 'Religious Musings', these lectures are full of Priestley, and espoused Priestley's curious combination of political agitation and cosmic faith, at once eager to change society while insisting that all things were well – for are not *all* things part of the one life of God? 'Reasoning strictly and with logical Accuracy I should deny the existence of any Evil', Coleridge told his audience, 'I have been able to discover nothing of which the end is not good'. He was developing ideas about God's presence in the world that would soon shape his nature poetry: 'The Omnipotent has unfolded to us the Volume of the World, that there we may read the Transcript of himself'.

This religious background to Coleridge's politics makes them importantly different from those of many of his contemporaries, such as Godwin, and Coleridge himself was keen to emphasise the difference. Of Godwin's *Political Justice*, for instance, he told his audience that 'whatever is just in it, is more forcibly recommended in the Gospel and whatever is new is absurd'. In later life, Coleridge would deny he had ever been a 'Jacobin', and, insofar as progressive politics at the time often went along with a rejection of Christian belief, he had a point. Where he made common cause with other voices on the political left was in the objects of his attack: poverty, the war against France, censorship, slavery. 'He has delivered many Lectures here', a Bristol journalist noticed appreciatively, 'one of which (on the Slave-trade) is a proof of the detestation in which he holds that infamous traffic'. Nevertheless, our correspondent added, 'Mr. C– would … do well to appear with cleaner stockings in public, and if his hair were combed out every time he appeared in public it would not depreciate him in the esteem of his friends'.

By the summer of 1795, Pantisocracy was in trouble. Southey, whose fervour was cooling, had suggested that the emigrants might postpone Pennsylvania for the time being and instead set up a farm in Wales. Coleridge was incredulous, but reluctantly conceded. Then, under pressure from his family, Southey toyed with the idea of becoming a minister in the Church of England. Again, Coleridge tried to sound reasonable about such back-sliding, reminding Southey about his latterly professed view of the established Church: 'you believe it iniquitous – mother of

Crimes!' Southey then briefly wondered about becoming a lawyer, before settling on a life of letters, and, having come into an annuity, he withdrew himself from the Pantisocrat enterprise altogether. Coleridge was splenetic and, in November, wrote a magnificently reproachful letter, surveying the history of their friendship and attacking Southey's weak principles: 'You are *lost* to *me*, because you are lost to Virtue'. Southey's infectious political enthusiasm had cost Coleridge everything: 'I abandoned my friends, and every prospect & every certainty, and the Woman whom I loved to an excess which you in your warmest dream of fancy could never shadow out'.

Coleridge's reference to Mary Evans in that letter is especially telling since at the time of writing he was newly married to Sara Fricker. Their wedding had taken place on 4 October 1795, in St Mary Redcliffe in Bristol. For their honeymoon, Coleridge had leased for several weeks a cottage in Clevedon, on the Bristol

St Mary Redcliffe, by John Sell Cotman (1802). In this church on 4 October 1795, Coleridge married Sara Fricker.

The British Museum, 1859-5-28-117

Channel, and from there he wrote excitedly to Thomas Poole, enthusing about the scenery – 'Mine Eye gluttonizes' – and declaring himself 'united to the woman, whom I love best of all created Beings'. He meant it too, for the couple had evidently grown genuinely close over the summer, at least if the electric crackle of the lines 'Written at Shurton Bars' is anything to go by.

The first of Coleridge's great poems, 'The Eolian Harp', is a Clevedon poem, set in the Somerset landscape, beside 'our cot o'ergrown | With white-flower'd Jasmin, and the broad-leav'd Myrtle'. It is a love poem, and also a poem about God's life in nature, as though the union of their marital love emulated in miniature the divine unity of the created world:

> *And what if all of animated nature*
> *Be but organic Harps diversely fram'd,*
> *That tremble into thought, as o'er them sweeps*
> *Plastic and vast, one intellectual Breeze,*
> *At once the Soul of each, and God of all?*

The Eolian harp was a favourite intellectual toy of the period. It comprised a wooden sounding-box with tuned strings across it which, when the instrument was placed in a sash-window, sounded in the breeze – rather a dreary noise, truth be told, but its music was much celebrated in poetry of the time as a symbol for the way the sensitive genius responds to the very subtlest of impressions, as the slightest breeze would stir the harp into music. In his poem Coleridge ingeniously uses it as a metaphor for the relationship between animate creatures (the harps) and the animating spirit of their God (the breeze) – an enticing thought, but one which Coleridge evidently recognised to be scarcely orthodox, for in the poem he has Sara's 'more serious eye' send him 'a mild reproof' for entertaining such theological audacities. Charles Lamb was much amused by the vignette of married life which that conjured up.

'The Eolian Harp' is a fine poem in itself, and the archetype of yet finer poems. It is the earliest example of what critics often call Coleridge's 'conversation' poems, a group which also includes, among others, 'This Lime-Tree Bower', 'Frost at Midnight' and 'The Nightingale'. (Coleridge himself collected together the works in question as 'Meditative Poems in Blank Verse'.) As the critics' label suggests, these poems all emulate a speaking voice, but they are also characterised by a common structure. Beginning with a keen-eyed description of a scene, the poems take an inward turn toward the workings of the mind and to the memories stirred in it by association; the poems then gather themselves toward a pitch of religious epiphany ('And what if all of animated nature ....?'), before completing a circle and returning to the outer scene again – the ordinary details of which are now invested with a sense of the spiritual, discovered in the course of the poems. This interweaving of natural objects and religious feeling would later feature in *Biographia Literaria* as one end of great poetry: 'to excite a feeling analogous to the supernatural, by awakening the mind's attention from the lethargy of custom, and directing it to the loveliness and the wonders of the world before us'. Coleridge recognised the innovation of his genre, and its influence on other poets: 'I have some claim to the thanks of no small number of the readers of poetry in having first introduced this species of short blank verse poems – of which Southey, Lamb, Wordsworth, and others have since produced so many exquisite specimens'. Wordsworth's 'Tintern Abbey', for one, is much indebted to Coleridge's example.

So Pantisocracy was dead, but Coleridge's radicalism was not finished, and he travelled back and forth between rural life in Clevedon and political life in Bristol. His ambiguous feelings about leaving the tranquillity of the countryside, and prosecuting 'the bloodless fight | Of Science, Freedom, and the Truth in Christ', form the subject of his next conversation poem, 'Reflections on Having Left a Place of Retirement'. He published a version of his political lectures as *Conciones ad Populum, or Addresses to the People*, and he returned to the platform to speak out against bills currently before parliament designed further to suppress opposition to the government.

Coleridge spent much of the early months of 1796 travelling in dissenting circles in the English midlands, gathering subscribers for a new journal to be entitled *The Watchman*, written and published by himself. The 'Prospectus' he carried with him prominently bore the potent motto which would appear on each title-page: 'That All may know the Truth; And that the Truth may make us Free!!' Coleridge

The front page of the second number of The Watchman, *which featured Coleridge's controversial essay on fasting.*

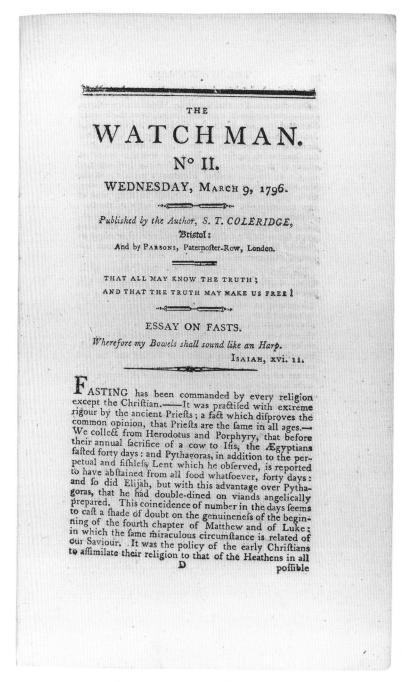

THE

WATCHMAN.

Nº II.

WEDNESDAY, MARCH 9, 1796.

Published by the Author, *S. T. COLERIDGE*, Bristol: And by PARSONS, Paternoster-Row, London.

THAT ALL MAY KNOW THE TRUTH; AND THAT THE TRUTH MAY MAKE US FREE!

ESSAY ON FASTS.

Wherefore my Bowels shall sound like an Harp.

ISAIAH, xvi. 11.

FASTING has been commanded by every religion except the Christian.——It was practised with extreme rigour by the ancient Priests; a fact which disproves the common opinion, that Priests are the same in all ages.—— We collect from Herodotus and Porphyry, that before their annual sacrifice of a cow to Isis, the Ægyptians fasted forty days: and Pythagoras, in addition to the perpetual and fishless Lent which he observed, is reported to have abstained from all food whatsoever, forty days: and so did Elijah, but with this advantage over Pythagoras, that he had double-dined on viands angelically prepared. This coincidence of number in the days seems to cast a shade of doubt on the genuineness of the beginning of the fourth chapter of Matthew and of Luke; in which the same miraculous circumstance is related of our Saviour. It was the policy of the early Christians to assimilate their religion to that of the Heathens in all

D   possible

passed on to a correspondent the response of one aristocrat, who upon seeing the motto exclaimed 'A *Seditious* beginning!' – evidently unaware, as Coleridge was pleased to note, that 'that *seditious* Dog was – JESUS CHRIST!' (Coleridge was quoting from the Gospel of John). *The Watchman* described itself, as would many of

Coleridge's prose works, as a 'miscellany', and when it began to appear in March, its miscellaneousness was very obvious. It included reports on current affairs and parliamentary debates, as well as poems and, in most numbers, an essay by Coleridge himself. These essays included a reworking of his successful slave-trade lecture, and a 'Remonstrance to the French Legislators', signalling Coleridge's growing wariness about the bloodiness of events in France. The second issue's essay protested against the national fast-days imposed by the Church. Nonconformist Christians, like Unitarians, normally took a dim view of fasting, which they saw as a symptom of ecclesiastical corruption, so this was a likely subject for Coleridge to address; and an opposition to fasts was further heightened by the propagandist prayers appointed to be read on the occasion, which petitioned God for success in the war against France. But Coleridge put at the head of his essay an epigraph from the Bible that made a risqué joke about flatulence – 'Wherefore my Bowels shall sound like an Harp' – which (he recalled) 'lost me near five hundred of my subscribers at one blow'. The journal closed after ten issues.

Coleridge's other publishing venture of the year, *Poems on Various Subjects*, which appeared in the spring, was much more successful. It contained, among other things, his sonnets, his address 'To a Young Ass', 'The Eolian Harp' (at this stage entitled 'Effusion XXXV'), and 'Religious Musings'; and it had sold out before the end of the year. The publisher was Joseph Cottle, a Bristol bookseller who had kept a kindly and bemused eye over the Pantisocrats, and had been generous with advances. Coleridge later grew exasperated by Cottle, and everyone made fun of his

POEMS

ON

VARIOUS SUBJECTS,

BY

S. T. COLERIDGE,

LATE OF JESUS COLLEGE, CAMBRIDGE.

Felix curarum, cui non Heliconia cord
Serta, nec imbelles Parnassi e vertice laurus:
Sed viget ingenium, et magnos accinctus in usus
Fert animus quascunque vices.—— Nos tristia vitæ
Solamur cantu.

STAT. SILV. Lib. iv. 4.

LONDON:

PRINTED FOR C. G. AND J. ROBINSONS, AND
J. COTTLE, BOOKSELLER, BRISTOL.

1796.

The title page of Poems on Various Subjects, *by* 'S.T. Coleridge, Late of Jesus College, Cambridge'. *Coleridge had finally abandoned his university career at the end of 1794.*

The British Library, C132.c.16

A cartoon of Joseph Cottle, Coleridge's publisher, made by Charles Lamb in a letter (c.1819) and signed 'C.L. fecit' (C.L. drew this). Lamb comments below the drawing: 'The lips should be a little thicker & perhaps the left eye has hardly justice done it but I should only spoil it by tampering with it'.

Courtesy Dent Publishers

poetry, especially his awful epic *Alfred*, but he played an important role in Coleridge's life, seeing not only Coleridge into print, but also Southey and Lamb and Wordsworth, often to his own financial disadvantage. Cottle's *Early Recollections* (1837), gossipy and unreliable as it is, remains our best account of Coleridge's life in Bristol in the 1790s.

The Coleridges' first child, David Hartley (later known simply as 'Hartley'), was born in September 1796, named after the English philosopher whose *Observations on Man* (1749) had much influenced the Unitarianism of Priestley. Coleridge had been thinking about setting up a school, but he now dropped the idea in favour of a life back in retirement, in which traces of the Pantisocratic ideal are not hard to detect: 'I am anxious that my children should be bred up from earliest infancy in the simplicity of peasants, their food, dress, and habits completely rustic'. So, at the end of 1796, the young family moved to Nether Stowey in Somerset, where they settled in a tiny cottage which Poole had found for them. (It is now a museum, and well worth a visit.) Behind the house, their garden met with the grounds of Poole's handsome townhouse: Coleridge dug the garden and gave himself calluses. He wrote to John Thelwall, one of the leading radicals of the age, celebrating the country life: 'We are *very* happy – & my little David Hartley grows a sweet boy – & has high health – he laughs at us till he makes us weep for very fondness'.

Coleridge busied himself writing a tragedy, *Osorio*, which he hoped to see performed at the Drury Lane theatre (a revised version would be staged successfully in 1813), and he prepared a second edition of his *Poems*, to be published again by Cottle. This time, besides his own work, the volume contained poems by Charles

Lamb and by a new member of Coleridge's circle, Charles Lloyd. Lloyd was the child of a wealthy banking family and a devoted admirer of Coleridge and, for a time, he became a paying live-in disciple. He was not an easy member of a household for he was prone to violent seizures, possibly of an epileptic kind, and Coleridge found nursing him nerve-racking. In the spring of 1797, following an especially severe attack, Lloyd left for a sanatorium to try and recover his health. Coleridge was exhausted, suffering 'a depression too dreadful to be described', as he told Cottle.

Coleridge's cottage in Nether Stowey, as engraved by Edmund H. New (1913).

The British Library, 010826.i.12

～ *Wordsworth 1797–1799*

B ut soon, in late March or early April 1797, Coleridge had a welcome visitor. He had first met William Wordsworth in September 1795, in the handsome house of the Pinney family in Bristol. (The house still stands, now open to the public.) Wordsworth was friendly with the Pinney sons, who were active in Bristol radical life, and Coleridge, a prominent figure on the scene, would have been a natural guest at their house. 'I saw but little of him', Wordsworth wrote after their

William Wordsworth, by Robert Hancock (1798) – showing, perhaps, what Hazlitt saw in the young Wordsworth's face: 'an intense high narrow forehead, a Roman nose, cheeks furrowed by strong purpose and feeling, and a convulsive inclination to laughter about the mouth'.

The Wordsworth Trust

first encounter, 'I wished indeed to have seen more – his talent appears to me very great'. The poets evidently kept in touch, and by May 1796 Coleridge was referring to Wordsworth as a 'very dear friend' as well as 'the best poet of the age', and he was pleased to receive Wordsworth's high opinion of 'Religious Musings'. By this time, Wordsworth and his sister Dorothy were living in an elegant house in Racedown, Dorset, lent to them by the ever-hospitable Pinneys. Here, Wordsworth busied himself with *The Borderers*, an unwieldy tragedy that obliquely recorded the collapse of his revolutionary hopes in general and his disenchantment with Godwin in particular.

Wordsworth had travelled to Bristol to see Cottle and, walking back to Racedown, he called at Stowey where he found Coleridge in low spirits. The two of them talked about poetry and agreed about the shortcomings of Southey, which must have been cheering. To judge by a letter Coleridge wrote shortly afterwards, they talked too about how to write an epic. Coleridge passed on the specifications to Cottle, in a way hardly calculated to warm the heart of a publisher:

> *I should not think of devoting less than 20 years to an Epic Poem. Ten to collect materials and warm my mind with universal science. I would be a tolerable Mathematician, I would thoroughly know Mechanics, Hydrostatics, Optics, and Astronomy, Botany, Metallurgy, Fossilism, Chemistry, Geology, Anatomy, Medicine – then the mind of man – then the minds of men – in all Travels, Voyages and Histories. So I would spend ten years – the next five to the composition of the poem – and the five last to the correction of it.*

He is being funny here, but not just funny, as it was to be an important part of his literary theory that the imaginative mind synthesises quite diverse areas of knowledge and experience into new poetic wholes.

Coleridge had other things in common with Wordsworth beside an interest in epic. Coleridge was thinking about an 'answer to Godwin' as well as writing his tragedy, both pursuits which overlapped with Wordsworth's own. So it is not surprising that, a few weeks later, Coleridge thought to return the visit. He turned up at Racedown in the first days of June, and half a century later the Wordsworths still remembered his arrival: 'He did not keep to the high road, but leaped over a gate and bounded down a pathless field, by which he cut off an angle'. At the time, Dorothy wrote to a friend soon after Coleridge's visit: 'You had a great loss in not

seeing Coleridge. He is a wonderful man … His conversation teems with soul, mind, and spirit'. The poets read each other works in progress: first, Wordsworth's 'The Ruined Cottage'; then Coleridge recited what he had written of his tragedy, and Wordsworth responded with his own – 'absolutely wonderful', Coleridge excitedly reported back to Cottle, 'T. Poole's opinion of Wordsworth is – that he is the greatest Man, he ever knew – I coincide'. Coleridge was quite as taken with Dorothy: 'She is a woman indeed! – in mind, I mean, & heart … Her information various – her eye watchful in minutest observation of nature – and her taste a perfect electrometer'.

They spent most of the rest of the month at Racedown, and in early July Coleridge brought the Wordsworths to Stowey – just as Charles Lamb and his sister Mary turned up for a week's stay. The cottage must have been impossibly cramped, and the party seems to have spent as much time as possible outside, walking in the nearby Quantock Hills or reading beneath the trees. This is the time memorialised in 'This Lime-Tree Bower My Prison', a poem occasioned (as Coleridge told Southey, with whom he was on better terms again) by Sara emptying

a pan of boiling milk over his foot. Coleridge sat incapacitated in the bower where his garden met Poole's, and there he generously imagined a natural epiphany on Charles Lamb's behalf:

> *So my friend*
> *Struck with deep joy may stand, as I have stood,*
> *Silent with swimming sense; yea, gazing round*
> *On the wide landscape, gaze till all doth seem*
> *Less gross than bodily; and of such hues*
> *As veil the Almighty Spirit, when yet he makes*
> *Spirits perceive his presence.*

When Coleridge sent his lines to Southey, he added a note to this passage: 'You remember, I am a *Berkleian*' – the philosophy of Bishop Berkeley, which construed the whole world of sense experience as a testimony to God's existence, was Coleridge's new philosophical enthusiasm. Lamb might have sought the deepest calm that came

Above left:

A list of projected works from an early Coleridge notebook (1796). The third entry reads 'The Origin of Evil, an Epic Poem'. Also listed are an 'Essay on Bowles', 'Strictures on Godwin', and 'Pantisocracy, or a Practical Essay on the Abolition of Indivi[du]al Property'. (None of the works were ever written.)

The British Library, Add MS 27901 f. 21

with such a philosophy more eagerly than most, for the 'evil and pain | And strange calamity' which Coleridge mentions in the poem refers to the death of Lamb's mother, murdered by his sister during a fit of insanity less than a year before. (With heroic sacrifice, Lamb undertook to look after his sister, and would do so for the rest of his life.) The theological puzzle of pain and suffering had occupied Coleridge before that calamity, however, as well it might someone who held the world wholly replete with the goodness of God, and who propounded 'the wisdom & goodness of Nature'. He later formulated that religious puzzle as 'the Question of Evil' – 'woe to the man, to whom it is an uninteresting Question', he would write in his notebook. Much of his best poetry would return to that abiding and troubling question.

The loan of Racedown was about to expire, and Coleridge had Poole swiftly negotiate on the Wordsworths' behalf the lease of Alfoxden, a large and handsome house with its own deer park, close to Stowey, which Poole managed to secure for them at a very low rent – '*23£ a year, taxes included*!!' The Wordsworths moved there in July. Coleridge's admiration grew and grew: 'Wordsworth is a very great man', he told Southey, rather pointedly, 'the only man, to whom *at all times* & in *all modes of excellence* I feel myself inferior'. Coleridge and the Wordsworths walked in the park and in the surrounding woods, excursions recorded by Dorothy in her journal. It remains lovely country – as William Hazlitt said, 'beautiful, green and hilly, and near the sea-shore'.

'I am wearied with politics, even to soreness', Coleridge wrote to a friend, but it was not so easy to evade. Shortly after the Wordsworths moved in, John Thelwall, with whom Coleridge had corresponded, arrived for a stay. Thelwall, a radical of great courage, was also worn out by politics, and he found the rural existence quite

Opposite page, right:

A letter sent by Coleridge from Racedown to John Prior Estlin, a Unitarian friend, 10 June 1797. 'This is a lovely country – & Wordsworth is a great man.'

Bristol Central Library

Alfoxden Park, near Nether Stowey. William and Dorothy Wordsworth moved there in July 1797. Painting by C.W. Bampfylde.

The Wordsworth Trust

Samuel Taylor Coleridge

The two sides of a manuscript copy of 'Kubla Khan', with its celebrated first lines: 'In Xannadù did Cubla Khan \ A stately Pleasure-Dome decree.'

The British Library, Add MS 50847 f.1,1v

as soothing as Coleridge had described it. 'I said to him – "Citizen John! this is a fine place to talk treason in!"' as Coleridge later told the story. '"Nay, Citizen Samuel!" replied he, "it is a fine place to make a man forget that there is any necessity for treason"'. As it transpired, Thelwall had been followed by a government agent who, finding his quarry had already moved on, filed reports instead about the 'Sett of Violent Democrats' he found based about Alfoxden. In *Biographia Literaria*, Coleridge turns the event into a droll story about 'Spy Nozy': eavesdropping on Wordsworth and Coleridge talking about the philosopher *Spinoza*, the agent

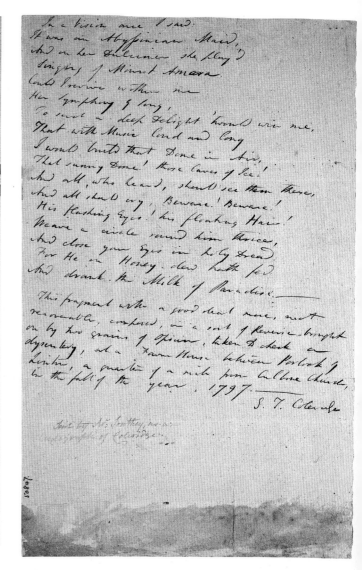

thought they were talking about him, a *nosy spy*. But at the time things were not so jolly, and Coleridge nervously put Thelwall off his plans to settle in the area: 'even riots & dangerous riots might be the consequence'. The British had been at war with France since 1793, by 1797 Holland and Spain had both joined with the French, and Britain expected an invasion at any moment. The political atmosphere was immensely tense, and life was increasingly difficult for anyone who might be thought to sympathise with the democratic declarations of the French republic.

Despite the burdensome political atmosphere – or perhaps because of it – Coleridge was beginning on his greatest period of poetry. In October, he finished his tragedy and sent it off to the politician and dramatist Richard Brinsley Sheridan, who was a partner in the Drury Lane Theatre, but Sheridan rejected it. In November, probably, he wrote 'Kubla Khan', 'composed', as Coleridge noted on a manuscript now in the British Library, 'in a sort of Reverie brought on by two grains of Opium, taken to check a dysentry, at a Farm House between Porlock & Linton'. The poem begins with an astonishing myth of creation, in which the Khan summons his dome into existence like God's *Fiat* creating light in Genesis: 'In Xanadu did Kubla Khan | A stately pleasure-dome decree'. The idea that the artist's imagination emulates God's would become central to Coleridge's literary thought, but in the poem, interestingly, such imaginative power is attributed to a famous tyrant. (The real Kublai Khan was a thirteenth century emperor of China, the grandson of Genghis Khan.) The poem is not just about the magnificent dome, but also about the relationship between the Khan's stately work of art and the untamed natural wilderness of Xanadu that surrounds it – 'that deep romantic chasm'. The centre of the poem is a fleeting reconciliation of the two opposed realms:

> *The shadow of the dome of pleasure*
> *Floated midway on the waves;*
> *Where was heard the mingled measure*
> *From the fountain and the caves.*
> *It was a miracle of rare device,*
> *A sunny pleasure-dome with caves of ice!*

Samuel Taylor Coleridge

Near Porlock, Somerset, *a watercolour by John White Abbott (1811). It was at a farmhouse between Porlock and Lynton that Coleridge wrote 'Kubla Khan'.*

Exeter City Museums and Art Gallery

It is as though Coleridge is anticipating the principle that he would later announce more abstractly in *Biographia Literaria* – that imagination 'reveals itself in the balance or reconciliation of opposite or discordant qualities'. But such a miracle is no sooner achieved in 'Kubla Khan' than it slips away: the last lines of the poem abruptly change direction, and the poet himself enters the frame for the first time – not a figure of Khan-like magnificence and authority, but someone needily hoping for the return of the 'Abyssinian maid'. She seems a sort of inspiring muse figure who has latterly forsaken him – 'Could I revive within me | Her symphony and song'. It is wholly Coleridgean that a resounding evocation of creative power should be swiftly followed by intimations of its failure. Later works, especially 'Dejection: An Ode', would embrace the failure of imagination yet more openly as a theme for poetry.

Later in November, while on an expedition to the village of Watchet in Somerset, Coleridge and Wordsworth worked out the plan of a ballad – there was a great vogue for ballads and they hoped to sell such a poem to a magazine and make some money. Coleridge's religious interest in the question of evil had already moved him to consider it a good subject for a poem, and he had recently attempted to compose a prose poem in collaboration with Wordsworth on the subject of Cain, the son of Adam who murdered his brother Abel. On their walk to Watchet there arose the idea of a ballad in which, as Wordsworth later recalled, 'some crime was to be committed which should bring upon the Old Navigator, as Coleridge afterwards delighted to call him, the spectral persecution, as a consequence of that crime, and his own wanderings'. Wordsworth suggested that the shooting of an albatross might serve as a crime – he had just been reading about such exotic creatures in George Shelvocke's *Voyage round the World by the Way of the Great South Sea* (1726), one episode of which features a sailor killing an albatross he thinks an unlucky omen. Collaboration on the new poem did not prosper any more than it had on *The Wanderings of Cain* – 'I soon found that the style of Coleridge and myself would not assimilate', Wordsworth later said. So Coleridge wrote on alone, finishing one version of 'The Ancient Mariner' before December, and, the following March, the earliest version that we have.

It is Coleridge's greatest work, the place where his sense of homelessness and abandonment – 'Alone, alone, all all alone, | Alone on the wide wide Sea' – combines most powerfully with his ability to imagine the redemption that he did not know. The watersnakes, which appear to the Mariner's eye as repulsive 'slimy things' in part II, become transformed at the end of part IV into blessed representatives of a universe of life:

> *O happy living things! no tongue*
> *Their beauty might declare:*
> *A spring of love gusht from my heart,*
> *And I bless'd them unaware!*
> *Sure my kind saint took pity on me,*
> *And I bless'd them unaware.*

The Mariner's nightmarish suffering is interrupted by a spontaneous act of benediction – rather as, at the end of 'This Lime-Tree Bower My Prison', the flicker of 'evil and pain | And strange calamity' is absorbed into the encompassing swell of Coleridge's blessing:

> *My gentle-hearted Charles! when the last rook*
> *Beat its straight path along the dusky air*
> *Homewards, I blest it! deeming its black wing*
> *(Now a dim speck, now vanishing in light)*
> *Had cross'd the mighty Orb's dilated glory,*
> *While thou stood'st gazing; or, when all was still,*
> *Flew creeking o'er thy head, and had a charm*
> *For thee, my gentle-hearted Charles, to whom*
> *No sound is dissonant which tells of Life.*

A rook, like a watersnake (or, indeed, an ass), is not nature at its most obviously winning: recognising that even such unattractive creatures live within the one encompassing life of God is a kind of revelation.

A simpler poem than 'The Ancient Mariner' might have made the happy moment with the watersnakes the turning point in a plot of crime and atonement: 'Sure my kind saint took pity on me' – but the power of Coleridge's ballad comes largely from the way it is very far from 'Sure' about the atonement it envisages. Coleridge leaves the Mariner's motive for shooting the albatross deliberately obscure, but there is no doubt about how the Mariner himself comes retrospectively to regard his action: he feels he has committed an act of fratricide, killing his brother in the family of Creation, and at the end of the poem he seems to have learned his lesson well, speaking warmly of the virtues of hospitality and the wisdom of loving equally all living things. But if he has learnt such a lesson, he does not seem to benefit from it much personally, for the poem comes to its close with the Mariner himself quite as lonely and cut off as ever. Through the poem, while he is telling his dreadful story, a wedding is being celebrated in the background, but the Mariner himself never participates in the festival or the communal life it represents. And he may even have made a convert to his life of isolation, since the last thing we see is the Wedding Guest turning away from 'the bridegroom's door'. The poem imagines a redemptive pattern to experience, which it does not manage quite to fulfil. No other work of Coleridge's gathers together so many of his central compulsions, and it is no wonder that he returned to it so obsessively, rewriting and revising it throughout his life.

Coleridge was badly in need of money and on the brink of accepting a job as a Unitarian minister when, in January 1798, he received the offer of an annuity from the philanthropic Wedgwood brothers, Josiah and Tom, the famous potters, whose acquaintance he had first made through Cottle. The Wedgwoods wrote to Coleridge, expressing their admiration for his 'character & abilities' and offering him 'an annuity for life of £150' with 'no conditions whatsoever being annexed to it', so as to secure his freedom for a life of the mind. 'Such benevolence is something so new, that I am not certain that I am not dreaming', wrote Coleridge. 'I hope the fruit will be good as the seed is noble', Wordsworth drily remarked. The young William Hazlitt, later one of the age's most prominent journalists and critics, was visiting Nether Stowey when the offer of the annuity came through. In his great essay 'My First Acquaintance with Poets' he remembers Coleridge making up his mind to accept the annuity while 'in the act of tying on one of his shoes'. Hazlitt vividly evokes Coleridge's conversation: 'In digressing, in dilating, in passing from subject to subject, he appeared to me to float in air, to slide on ice'. When he returned later in the year, Coleridge took him to meet the Wordsworths. Both poets recited their verses, and Hazlitt listened:

> *Coleridge's manner is more full, animated, and varied; Wordsworth's more equable, sustained, and internal. The one might be termed more dramatic, the other more lyrical. Coleridge has told me that he himself liked to compose in walking over uneven ground, or breaking through the straggling branches of a copsewood; whereas Wordsworth always wrote (if he could) walking up and down a strait gravel-walk, or in some spot where the continuity of his verse met with no collateral interruption.*

William Hazlitt's self-portrait (1802). Hazlitt would later become a fierce critic of Coleridge's growing conservatism, but his essay 'My First Acquaintance with Poets' offers the most sympathetic and vivid glimpse of the young Coleridge at the height of his poetic powers.

Maidstone Museum and Art Gallery, Kent/ Bridgeman Art Gallery

It was the poets' most wonderful year, a period retrospectively cast in Wordsworth's *Prelude* as a golden summer of collaboration:

> *That summer when on Quantock's grassy hills*
> *Far ranging, and among the sylvan combs,*
> *Thou in delicious words, with happy heart,*
> *Didst speak the vision of that Ancient Man,*
> *The bright-eyed Mariner, and rueful woes*
> *Didst utter of the Lady Christabel …*

Coleridge's immense productivity continued: he was writing the first (and best) part of 'Christabel'. In that poem, as in 'The Ancient Mariner', Coleridge set his story in an imagined world of supersitition and medieval Catholicism, adopting its language to portray the destruction of goodness – as though he were fascinated by

The Valley of Rocks, Lynton *(1820s–1830s), a watercolour by George Robert Lewis. Coleridge brought Hazlitt here and in 'My First Acquaintance with Poets' Hazlitt recalled 'a place…bedded among precipices overhanging the sea, with rocky caverns beneath, into which the waves dash, and where the sea-gull for ever wheels its screaming flight'.*

The British Museum 1883.10.13.36

49

An early notebook of Coleridge's, open to show an entry describing Hartley (c.1797–98). 'The Moon caught his eye – he ceased crying immediately – & his eyes & the tears in them, how they glittered in the Moonlight!'

an evil which his official theology could not properly comprehend. 'Christabel' portrays the ruinous vulnerability of its main character's blue-eyed innocence before the dangerous enchantments of the witch-like Geraldine: 'Hush, beating heart of Christabel! | Jesu, Maria, shield her well!' The moral is not simple, however, for, like the Mariner, Geraldine seems as much the victim as she is the agent of her own wrong-doing. The poem inhabits a darkly confused Coleridgean underworld, troubling the Unitarian buoyancy that had lately filled his lectures and philosophical poetry.

That optimistic vision is more nearly expressed in 'Frost at Midnight', perhaps the finest of all the conversation poems, also written at this time. Here, innocence is benevolently watched over and protected: Coleridge tenderly imagines for his son a childhood of untroubled naturalness spent among 'The lovely shapes and sounds intelligible | Of that eternal language, which thy God | Utters'. The childhood foreseen looks very like a version of Wordworth's, spent in a Lake District that Coleridge had yet to see: '*thou*, my babe! shalt wander like a breeze | By lakes and sandy shores, beneath the crags | Of ancient mountain'. (The only darkness in the poem is the recollected deprivation of Coleridge's own childhood.)

'Fears in Solitude', 'France: An Ode' and 'The Nightingale' also come from this time, the last based on one of many episodes in the early life of Hartley that Coleridge lovingly entered in his notebook:

> *– Hartley fell down & hurt himself – I caught him up crying &*
> *screaming – & ran out of doors with him. – The Moon caught his*
> *eye – he ceased crying immediately – & his eyes & the tears in*
> *them, how they glittered in the Moonlight!*

From about this time, Coleridge's notebook becomes his constant companion, to which he confided observations, thoughts, pen–portraits, aphorisms, scraps of poetry, plans for works, anecdotes, jokes, riddles and puns, as well as noting passages from books and conversations, and, more practically, times of appointments and calculations of debts. By the time Coleridge died, he had used some seventy or so notebooks of different shapes and sizes to record (as he put it) 'the history of my own mind'. Taken together, in the incomparable edition of Kathleen Coburn (who turned the immense jumble of papers into something readable), they constitute one of the most remarkable works of the romantic period. (The majority of the notebooks are now held by the British Library.)

Wordsworth was writing about children too, in 'We Are Seven', and about the creative workings of the mind, in 'The Thorn' and 'Goody Blake and Harry Gill'. He was meditating much grander things as well. Conversation with Coleridge had borne fruit in a projected epic about Nature, Man, and Society to be called *The Recluse*. Coleridge had himself toyed with a similar idea for a work to be entitled *The Brook*, a large-scale conversation poem which would blend meditative reflections and natural description, but it had not progressed beyond some fragments in his notebook. *The Recluse* now assumed the immense burden of Coleridge's epic ambitions, a poem to establish Wordsworth as Milton's successor, 'the first & greatest philosophical Poet'. Coleridge would watch with proprietary interest as Wordsworth struggled with his burdensome commission over the years.

The Wordsworths learnt that the lease of Alfoxden was not going to be renewed, and the circle discussed the idea of a trip to Germany. Coleridge judged such an excursion 'of high importance to my intellectual utility', mindful of the philosophical masterwork that the Wedgwoods were expecting of him, and Wordsworth agreed it would be good to know German. John Chester, a devotee of Coleridge's, would accompany them. Originally, Sara was to go too, but that plan was dropped, for finances were tight and a second boy had been born in May. The baby was named Berkeley, after Coleridge's latest philosophical passion. He enjoyed 'the paternal beauty in his upper lip', reported his proud father.

Money was required for the trip, and Coleridge floated various ideas past Cottle. In the end, the *Lyrical Ballads* emerged, a volume containing 'The Ancient Mariner' and 'The Nightingale', and some snippets from Coleridge's tragedy, along with several Wordsworth poems written in the spring of 1798, as well as some earlier works, and 'Tintern Abbey', which was written as the book went to press. Coleridge suggests in *Biographia Literaria* that the book was organised by a governing plan, but it is really a very diverse affair, and an unlikely candidate to inaugurate a literary revolution. *Lyrical Ballads* appeared in September 1798, with an advertisement announcing itself as an experiment 'to ascertain how far the language of conversation in the middle and lower classes of society is adapted to the purposes of poetic pleasure'. The reviews were reasonably good, although Southey grumpily announced himself unimpressed by much of it, and drubbed 'The Ancient Mariner' as 'a Dutch attempt at German sublimity'. He was one of the few who knew who the authors were, as *Lyrical Ballads* had appeared anonymously. Coleridge had explained to Cottle: 'Wordsworth's name is nothing – to a large number of persons mine *stinks*'.

Coleridge did put his name to another book, though, which he hastily contracted as he passed though London on the way to Yarmouth. The volume, *Fears in Solitude*, contained only three poems: the title-poem, which cherished the beauty of Stowey in the face of threatened French invasion; 'France: An Ode', in which

Coleridge publicly renounced his old sympathies with France; and 'Frost at Midnight', which found in the English landscape a path to divine revelation. It was an idiosyncratically patriotic publication, sent to press as he was leaving Britain's shores for the first time.

The anonymous title page of Lyrical Ballads, with a Few Other Poems *(1798).*

The British Library, C58.c.12/1

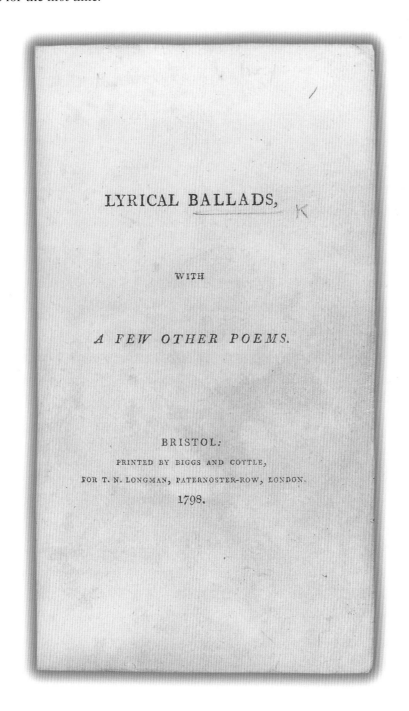

Coleridge recorded the sea journey to Germany in his notebook, remarking the strength of his constitution with pride: 'Chester was ill the Whole time – Wordsworth shockingly ill! – Miss Wordsworth worst of all – vomiting & groaning & crying the whole time! – And I the whole time as well as I ever was – neither sick or giddy'. While his companions were indisposed, Coleridge was taken up by a group of admiring Danes, one of whom drunkenly acclaimed him: 'Vat imagination! vat language! vat fast science! vat eyes! – vat a milk vite forehead! – O my Heafen! You are a God!' Once arrived in Hamburg, the poets secured a meeting with the aged Friedrich Klopstock, author of the epic *Messias*, who managed to speak to Wordsworth in French, 'but shewed no great depth in any thing' thought Coleridge. The party travelled on to Hamburg, 'an ugly City', in Coleridge's view, 'that stinks in every corner, house, & room worse than Cabbin, Sea sickness, or bilge Water'.

At the end of September, the Wordsworths split off to seek cheaper lodgings and they settled in the picturesque town of Goslar, in Lower Saxony, which was isolated but inexpensive. Here, after an aborted attempt at *The Recluse*, Wordsworth fell instead to writing his verse-autobiography, a sort of preamble to the philosophical epic that Coleridge expected of him. (This autobiographical poem, which was addressed to Coleridge, went through decades of revision and expansion and finally appeared after Wordsworth's death under the editorial title of *The Prelude*.) Meanwhile, Coleridge travelled with Chester to Ratzeburg; he wrote long chatty, sometimes homesick, journal-letters to Sara, describing the scenery and the meals and the eccentricities of continental life ('All the men have a hideous custom of picking their Teeth with their forks'); and he settled down to learn German, filling his notebook with lists of vocabulary. He planned a book about the dramatist and critic Gotthold Lessing. The winter closed in, the worst for a century. Coleridge noticed how its severity had slowed things down, even the kingfisher, 'its slow short flight permitting you to observe all its colours, almost as if it had been a flower'.

Back in England, little Berkeley died of consumption on 10 February 1799. Poole at first thought it best to keep the news from Coleridge, but eventually wrote to tell him. Coleridge wrote his wife a religious letter, seeking consolation in Unitarian thoughts: 'the living God is every where, & works every where – and where is there room for Death?', and he cautiously expressed a hope that their sense of loss might prove 'the foundations of a lasting love'. It is the first clear sign that the marriage had been under strain, exacerbated no doubt by Coleridge's recent time-consuming devotion to the Wordsworths.

In February, Coleridge enrolled at the University of Göttingen, rediscovering the pleasures of student life: 'Such an Evening I never passed before – roaring, kissing, embracing, fighting, smashing bottles & glasses against the wall, singing – in short, such a scene of uproar I never witnessed before, no, not even at Cambridge', he wrote home, adding nobly, 'I drank nothing'. (Sara was not impressed by what she heard about the parties.) He reported to Poole that the professors paid him the most '*flattering* attention'. But Coleridge was a tourist as well as a student, and in the spring, with a group of other Englishmen, he walked in the picturesque Hartz mountains. His letters describe the scenery sublimely: the hills were 'a Sea of huge motionless waves / too multiform for Painting, too multiform even for the Imagination to remember them / yea, my very sight seemed *incapacitated* by the novelty & Complexity of the Scene'. The loquacious memoirs of Clement Carlyon, one of the party, candidly offer some less imposing snapshots: 'I have heard him say, fixing his prominent eyes upon himself (as he was wont to do, whenever there was a mirror in the room), with a singularly coxcomical expression of countenance, that his dress was sure to be lost sight of the moment he began to talk; an assertion which, whatever may be thought of its modesty, was not without truth'. Coleridge wrote to the Wedgwoods assuring them that his studies were proceeding apace: 'I have worked harder than, I trust in God Almighty, I shall ever have occasion to work again ... I shall have bought 30 pounds worth of books (chiefly metaphysics / & with a view to the one work, to which I hope to dedicate in silence the prime of my life)'.

≈ *The Lakes 1799–1804*

The Wordsworths had returned to England in May 1799, fed up with Germany, and gone to stay with childhood friends, Tom Hutchinson and his sisters Mary, Sara and Joanna, at Tom's farm in Sockburn-on-Tees in the north-east of England. Coleridge was back in Stowey in late July. Relations with Southey were on an even keel again, and they began to plan a collaborative epic in hexameters about the prophet Mahomet and went on a brief walking tour. On his return to Stowey Coleridge found that Hartley had caught scabies, though he seemed quite untroubled, even by the smelly sulphurous treatment, during the application of which (Coleridge reported) he kept 'singing or chanting – I be a funny Fellow, And my name is Brimstonello'. Coleridge retreated 'as undisturbed as a Toad in a Rock' into the works of Spinoza, the seventeenth-century philosopher whose compelling pantheism Coleridge could neither fully accept nor wholly resist. He had summarised Spinoza's thought for his friends in Germany, as Clement Carlyon recalled: 'Each thing has a life of its own, and we are all one life' – which makes it sound very like the position expressed in 'Religious Musings' and 'The Eolian Harp'.

But thoughts of Wordsworth were not far away: 'I long to see what you have been doing', Coleridge wrote to him in October, 'O let it be the tail-piece of "The Recluse!" for of nothing but "The Recluse" can I hear patiently'. Then, abruptly, on 22 October, without warning Sara, he travelled north to Sockburn with Cottle, summoned (he subsequently claimed) by an alarm about Wordsworth's health. The Wordsworths had obviously been telling the Hutchinsons all about their remarkable friend, as, following his arrival, Coleridge wrote in his notebook: 'Few moments in life so interesting as those of an affectionate reception from those who have heard of you yet are strangers to your person'.

After a few days, Wordsworth, Coleridge and Cottle set off on a tour. Cottle, who was not vigorous, soon left them to return south, and the poets pressed on alone, heading west towards the Lake District. Over the next three weeks they circumnavigated the region, from Windermere to Bassenthwaite, and Ennerdale to Ullswater, for some of the time joined by Wordsworth's brother John. 'Your

Br[other] John is one of you', Coleridge wrote to Dorothy, offering high praise, 'a man who hath solitary usings of his own Intellect, deep in feeling, with a subtle Tact, a swift instinct of Truth & Beauty'. 'Coleridge enchanted with Grasmere and Rydal', Wordsworth reported back approvingly to Dorothy – as indeed he was: 'I cannot express for myself … how deeply I have been impressed by a world of scenery absolutely new to me'. The notebook is full of his palpable excitement, scribbled in present-tense, on-the-spot pencil. He was always alive to the activity of light, and the Lake country provided an unrivalled repertoire of effects: 'Exquisite Network of Film so instinct with gentle motion which, now the Shower only steadies, & now it melts it into such a mistiness as the Breath leaves on a mirror'.

The poets came to the town of Keswick, where Coleridge found waiting for him a letter from Daniel Stuart, proprietor of the *Morning Post*, offering him work; and when he parted company from Wordsworth on 18 November, it was with the intention of heading south to take it up at once. The second part of Wordsworth's autobiography bade him a fond, quietly anxious farewell:

> *Fare thee well:*
> *Health and the quiet of a healthful mind*
> *Attend thee, seeking oft the haunts of men –*
> *But yet more often living with thyself,*
> *And for thyself – so haply shall thy days*
> *Be many, and a blessing to mankind.*

But instead of heading for London, Coleridge returned to Sockburn, now alone, where he stayed with the Hutchinsons for a week, during which time he fell in love with Sara Hutchinson. His passion for her would dominate the next decade or more of his life, depriving him of anything like the quiet of a healthful mind. The entries made in the notebook at the time of his second visit to Sockburn are discreet, but one entry stands out: 'The long Entrancement of a True-love's Kiss'. Later, in Latin code, Coleridge returned to that time more expansively: 'pressed Sara's hand a long time behind her back, and then, then for the first time, loved pricked me with its light arrow, poisoned alas! and hopeless' – there is more, but it is heavily inked out.

Sara was in some ways an unlikely love-object, by all accounts rather plain and far from statuesque: a puzzled Mrs Coleridge thought her unexceptional, anyway. Coleridge mulled over the odd allure of the unextraordinary love-object in his notebook, perhaps with Sara Hutchinson in mind: 'Can see nothing extraordinary in her – a Poem noting all the virtues of the mild & retired kind'.

After his week at Sockburn, Coleridge finally caught the night coach to London. He woke to watch the sky at dawn, which he described in the notebook:

> *I saw Starlings in vast Flights, borne along like smoke, mist – like a body unindued with voluntary Power / – now it shaped itself into a circular area, inclined – now they formed a Square – now a Globe – now from complete Orb into an Ellipse – then oblongated into a Balloon with the Car suspended, now a concave Semicircle; still expanding, or contracting, thinning or condensing, now glimmering and shivering, now thickening, deepening, blackening!*

London struck him as harsh and unmoveable, compared 'with the universal motion of things in Nature'; but, for all his outspoken love of the countryside, Coleridge usually thrived in cities. Now he took lodgings off the Strand, and quickly established himself as a prominent journalist, writing for the *Morning Post* – his wittily hostile account of Prime Minister Pitt was especially admired. He renewed his intimacy with Lamb, and befriended William Godwin and the brilliant young chemist Humphry Davy; he charmed the actress 'Perdita' Robinson, and mixed with literary ladies. He attended the theatre and the House of Commons; he met publishers and landed a commission to translate the German playwright Schiller. Sara and Hartley joined him in early December, Hartley lively as ever, as Coleridge confirmed in a letter to Southey: 'To morrow Sara & I dine at Mister Gobwin's as Hartley calls him–who gave the philosopher such a Rap on the shins with a ninepin that Gobwin in huge pain *lectured* Sara on his boisterousness'.

But for all the distractions of the metropolitan scene, he was missing Wordsworth's company, and he was back in the Lakes in April. 'Coleridge has left us, to go into the North', wrote a dejected Lamb, 'on a visit to his God, Wordsworth'. The Wordsworths were by now set up in a house of their own: they had moved to Dove Cottage at the end of 1799, and Coleridge marked his arrival there with an entry in the notebook: 'Arrived at Grasmere April 6 – 1800'. (Dove Cottage is now a fine museum, an absorbing visit for anyone interested in Coleridge.) Coleridge was toiling with his translation of Schiller, 'irksome & soul-wearying Labor', and he still

The earliest existing image of Dove Cottage, by Amos Green (1806). The Wordsworths moved to the cotttage in the hamlet of Town End, a little to the south of Grasmere, at the end of 1799; Coleridge paid his first visit in April the following year.

The Wordsworth Trust

owed the Wedgwood brothers a book about Lessing and greater things besides. But for the time being he threw himself into a new enterprise: a second edition of *Lyrical Ballads*. He made many changes to his own 'Ancient Mariner', the pseudo-medieval spelling of which ('The Ancyent Marinere') had, in Wordsworth's view, 'upon the whole been an injury to the volume' – its appearance had certainly come as a surprise after Wordsworth's 'Advertisement' to the volume had announced an experiment in the poetical use of 'the language of conversation'.

Although he was unwilling to lose the company of Poole, Coleridge began to contemplate settling permanently in the Lake Country: 'if I cannot procure a suitable house at Stowey', he wrote to Godwin at the end of the month, 'I return to Cumberland & settle at Keswick – in a house of such prospect, that if … impressions & ideas *constitute* our Being, I shall have a tendency to become a God – so sublime & beautiful will be the series of my visual existence'. The house in question was Greta Hall, which commanded a fine position by the river Greta, with views of Derwentwater and the Skiddaw range of fells. The Wordsworths successfully negotiated the lease on Coleridge's behalf, and in June Coleridge arrived back in the Lakes with his family. His notebook recorded the momentous day: 'Re-arrived at Grasmere June 29th, 1800, on a Sunday, with wife and child'. They stayed with the Wordsworths in Dove Cottage for a little less than a month, while Coleridge and the others were busy working on the new edition of *Lyrical Ballads*. Coleridge walked in his new country, quickly assuming a resident's distaste for tourists: 'Ladies reading Gilpin's &c while passing by the very places instead of looking at the places'. (William Gilpin's was the leading picturesque guide book to the area.)

The Coleridges finally moved into Greta Hall on 24 July. Coleridge's letters celebrated his new location: 'I question, if there be a room in England which commands a view of Mountains & Lakes & Woods & Vales superior to that, in which I am now sitting'. It was a substantial house, let on generous terms by one William Jackson, who occupied rooms at the back. (It still stands, a private residence which you can peer at through iron gates, though now it is surrounded by other houses.) It is some thirteen miles away from Grasmere, a stiff but magnificent walk over the mountain range that looks down upon Thirlmere: a route which Coleridge would often take.

Once settled in Cumberland, he immediately became an enthusiastic fell-walker, climbing the mountains of Helvellyn, Scafell and Skiddaw in the first few weeks. Sometimes William and John Wordsworth joined him on excursions. He always carried his pocket notebook, recorded sightings and adventures, noting routes

Keswick Lake and Skiddaw, *a water-colour by Francis Towne (1786).* 'Keswick Lake' is *Derwentwater.*

Leeds City Art Gallery

View at Langdale *by John Constable (1806). Coleridge walked with William and John Wordsworth to Stickle Tarn, on the Langdales, on 2 September 1800, one of many excursions of the period which Coleridge recorded in his notebook.*

Victoria and Albert Museum

and place-names, jotting maps and scribbling drawings when dumbstruck: 'no–no! no words can convey any idea of this prodigious wildness'. Hartley was thriving too: 'all Health & extacy – He is a Spirit dancing on an aspen Leaf – unwearied in Joy, from morning to night indefatigably joyous'. On 14 September 1800, he gained a brother. Coleridge thought about calling the child Bracy, the name of the bard in 'Christabel', but they settled on Derwent, the name of the river near Greta Hall. The baby was not well, making (Coleridge noted) 'a noise exactly like the Creeking of a door which is being shut very slowly to prevent its creeking', but he recovered and was soon a 'very Stout Boy indeed'.

'Christabel' was on his mind as he was working hard to finish it for the new *Lyrical Ballads*, and he read the second part to the Wordsworths on 4 October. They declared themselves delighted with it, and pleased yet more the next day when it was read again; but the poem was still unfinished, and Dorothy succinctly noted in her journal for 6 October, 'Determined not to print Christabel with the LB'. 'I found that the Style of this Poem was so discordant from my own that it could not be printed along with my poems with any propriety', Wordsworth told their publisher:

instead, it would appear in another book, alongside a piece of Wordsworth's called 'The Pedlar' (but, in the end, this never happened).

The new edition of *Lyrical Ballads* appeared in early 1801. It was now in two volumes, with the second consisting of new poems by Wordsworth, who also contributed a lengthy Preface which defended the use of 'the real language of men' in verse. 'The Preface contains our joint opinions on Poetry', Coleridge said, and later acknowledged it 'half a child of my own Brain', but he would come firmly to disapprove of some of its main principles – his points of difference would, in time, give rise to the long discussion of Wordsworth in his *Biographia Literaria*. Wordsworth's name appeared alone on the title-page, though Wordsworth referred in his Preface to poems by 'a Friend'. 'The Ancient Mariner' had been moved from prime position to a more obscure corner, tucked in at the back of volume one just before 'Tintern Abbey', and Wordsworth

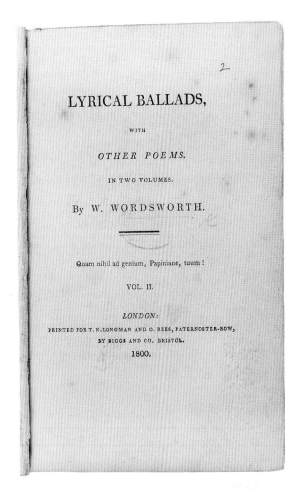

had supplied an oddly judged note which listed the several defects of his friend's poem. There is nothing to suggest that these decisions were not wholly consensual, but either way Coleridge was now thinking of the *Lyrical Ballads* as Wordsworth's property. Coleridge's faith in himself as a poet was shaken: 'As to Poetry, I have altogether abandoned it', he told Thelwall, 'being convinced that I never had the essentials of poetic Genius, & that I mistook a strong desire for original power'. He wrote to Godwin, suggesting what might be written about him in the event of his death: 'by shewing to him what true Poetry was, [Wordsworth] made him know, that he himself was no Poet'. In fact, Coleridge would continue to write poetry throughout his life, and endlessly revised many of his old poems; but it is true that his greatest period of poetry was over. He had been 'in blossom', as Wordsworth later put it, for about four years.

The title page of the second edition of Lyrical Ballads, *published in the first weeks of 1801 but dated 1800. Wordsworth appears as the single author.*

The British Library, C58.c.12

Talking about his death was melodramatic, but Coleridge really was often badly ill now. The Lake District scenery was thrilling, but its climate was unforgiving, and his health soon suffered. As a schoolboy, Coleridge had once let his clothes dry on his back after swimming, which had laid him up for weeks with a fever, and, according to his friend and biographer James Gillman, he dated from that time 'those bodily sufferings which embittered the rest of his life, and rendered it truly one of sickness and suffering'. From the later months of 1800 onwards, illness becomes a recurrent theme in the letters and notebooks: 'all sorts of crazinesses, blood-shot eyes, swoln Eye lids, rheumatic pains in the back of my head & limbs, clusters of Boils in my neck, &c'; rheumatic fever, a hydrocele, 'nephritic pains in my back which almost alternated with the stomach fits' – all of which necessitated 'the use of the Brandy & Laudanum'. Coleridge identified the underlying disease as gout, but many of the symptoms were probably the result of the opium, or temporary withdrawal from the opium, which he took as treatment. It is from this period that Coleridge himself later dated his own addiction to the drug, though he had taken laudanum (a preparation of opium) since Cambridge days – that was not at all unusual, since opium was the only available painkiller. As luck would have it, the local preparation in the Lakes, Kendal Black Drop, was supposed to be especially potent.

'My health is very, very bad', he wrote to Thelwall in April 1801, 'indeed, I feel & know, that (at all events, if I stay in this climate) I am going down to the Grave'. To Humphry Davy, he lamented: '"*Sinking, sinking, sinking*! I feel, that I am *sinking*!" … *Gout* in a young man of 29 – !' The state of his health could not have helped his marriage. Coleridge bluntly told Southey, 'we are not suited to each another'; and, in November, 'If my wife loved me, and I my wife, half as well as we both love our children, I should be the happiest man alive – but this is not – will not be!'. The Wordsworths seem unquestioningly to have taken Coleridge's line on Sara's shortcomings: 'She would have made a very good wife to many another man, but for Coleridge!! Her radical fault is want of sensibility and what can such a woman be to Coleridge', lamented Dorothy, 'She is to be sure a sad fiddle faddler'. Unsurprisingly, Sara regarded the Wordsworths with less than the spontaneous affection her husband expected.

Coleridge left Keswick in late 1801, and, after a Christmas break in Stowey with Poole, he resumed a London life. He wrote for the newspapers again, attended Humphry Davy's celebrated chemical lectures at the Royal Institution, and mixed with the literati. He was still sick with dreadful bowels (a symptom of opium addiction), about which he faithfully reported back north: 'We were made very unhappy', Dorothy wrote after one such letter arrived. But by February 1802 he was able to tell Poole that his health was

The manuscript of Coleridge's verse 'Letter to Sara Hutchinson', dated 4 April 1802 (later the basis for 'Dejection: An Ode'). 'Well! if the Bard was weatherwise, who made | The grand old Ballad of Sir Patrick Spence…'.

'on the Mend' and he had taken no 'opiates of any kind'. His spirits were improving too: 'I am quite a man of *fashion* – so many titled acquaintances', he told his wife, as usual growing fonder of her the longer they remained apart: 'I shall return in Love & chearfulness, & therefore in pleasurable Convalescence, if not in Health'.

Then, on the last day of February, 1802, he picked up news that Sara Hutchinson was ill, and he headed north at once to her bedside at Gallow Hill, near Scarborough, where she was staying with her brother. He stayed there for ten days before moving on to Greta. The trees were coming into leaf, as he recorded in his notebook: 'The Larches in spring push out their separate bundles of Leaves first into green Brushes or Pencils, which soon then are only small tassels'. By early April, things had reached a kind of crisis. 'I was, if possible, more miserable than before', he recalled afterwards, and his growing despair and bad health spilled over into a verse letter addressed to Sara Hutchinson.

His noticing of the larches gets into the poem ('The Larch, which pushes out in tassels green | It's bundled Leafits') as does his marvelling eye for luminescence ('the western Sky | And it's peculiar Tint of Yellow Green'); but such visible beauties now testify only to a crippling imaginative lack. Gazing at the moon and stars, rather as Charles Lamb had gazed upon the swimming landscape in 'This Lime-Tree Bower', Coleridge now finds himself experiencing, not epiphany, but an inner deadness: 'I see them all, so excellently fair! | I see, not feel, how beautiful they are'. In 'The Eolian Harp', his marriage had symbolised a wider harmony in creation, voiced by the wind harp's music; but in the 'Letter' to Sara, things are out of joint and the windharp screams tunelessly. His marriage has become the bleak opposite of proper union and concord, broken by 'habitual Ills | That wear out Life, when two unequal Minds | Meet in one House'. In an eminently Coleridgean way, personal devastation is mixed up with philosophical upheaval: Coleridge's loss of the 'shaping Spirit of Imagination' paradoxically empowers him to realise the power of the imagination that has deserted him. His Unitarian faith – that all things existed within the divine one life of God – was giving way to a new thought, that all things lived only within the subjective eye of the imagination:

> *O Sara! we receive but what we give,*
>
> *And in* our *Life alone does Nature live.*
>
> *Our's is her wedding garment, our's her Shroud –*
>
> *And would we aught behold of higher Worth*
>
> *Than that inanimate cold World allow'd*
>
> *To the poor loveless ever-anxious Crowd,*
>
> *Ah! from the Soul itself must issue forth*
>
> *A Light, a Glory, and a luminous Cloud*
>
> *Enveloping the Earth!*

It is as though the earlier position has been turned on its head. In 'The Eolian Harp', the individual self had been essentially passive, acted upon like a wind harp before the breeze, but Coleridge was now coming to believe that the mind was not (as he put it in a letter to Poole) 'a lazy Looker-on on an external World', but rather 'made in God's Image, & that too in the sublimest sense – the Image of the *Creator*' – and consequently that 'any system built on the passiveness of the mind must be false'. The 'life' of nature in 'Dejection' is not something divine in which Coleridge is passively immersed, but something which he projects onto his surroundings – or, rather, fails to project, in which case, in the absence of the life-giving gaze of imagination, the objects of his perception remain reproachfully 'inanimate' and 'cold'.

On 20 April, Coleridge walked over the fells to Dove Cottage, and the next day he read his verse-letter to Sara to the dismayed Wordsworths. After hearing the lines, Dorothy wrote in her journal: 'I was affected with them & was on the whole, not being well, in miserable spirits. The sunshine – the green fields & the fair sky made me sadder; even the little happy sporting lambs seemed but sorrowful to me'. On 4 October 1802, Coleridge published a version of the poem in the *Morning Post* as 'Dejection: An Ode', pruned of its more explicit references to his discordant home life, and with 'Sara' discreetly replaced by 'Lady'. But the association of the poem with his unhappy marriage would not have been lost on at least one reader. The poem appeared on the day Wordsworth married Sara Hutchinson's sister, Mary. It was Coleridge's wedding anniversary.

And yet it was not a period of unrelieved misery. The collapse in his spirits and health in April seemed to work a kind of reconciliation between Coleridge and his wife. His less than generous interpretation was that 'the thought of separation wounded her Pride', but anyway he was pleased to report to Southey 'more Love & Concord in my House, than I have known for years before', and he was suddenly fruitful again, one of a series of remarkable physical and mental resurrections that punctuate his story. Publicly, his career as a journalist was blossoming with important articles in the *Morning Post* about Napoleon and the political scene, and, toward the end of the year, a popular hit in the story of Mary the Beauty of Buttermere, whose seduction by a trickster posing as a Member of Parliament was one of the scandalous sensations of the day. Meanwhile, in the privacy of his correspondence, and in the wake of the philosophical re-orientation shown in the 'Letter to Sara Hutchinson', he was beginning to formulate the literary theory that would later appear in *Biographia Literaria*, including its important and influential distinction between Fancy and Imagination. The terms are synonymous in much eighteenth-century criticism, but Coleridge came to think them 'two distinct and widely different faculties'. Fancy forces ideas into poetic similes merely by arbitrary association – an 'aggregating Faculty of the mind', as he called it in a letter. But the Imagination synthesises diverse ideas into new wholes, a fully '*modifying*, and *co-adunating* Faculty'. ('Co-adunating' means 'bringing into one', like a marriage.) The imaginative poet, as Coleridge would later write in *Biographia Literaria*, 'diffuses a tone, and spirit of unity, that blends, and (as it were) *fuses*, each into each'.

Such speculations about the imagination went along with Coleridge's growing awareness of his divergence from Wordsworth. Coleridge was beginning to conceive of poetry as the exalted medium of the most eminent human faculties, and he was, accordingly, less and less inclined to endorse Wordsworth's claim in the Preface to *Lyrical Ballads* that there was no '*essential* difference between the language of Prose and metrical composition'. The new poems Wordsworth had been writing over the summer troubled Coleridge a good deal, precisely because of their daring proximity to what seemed unpoetical: he discerned 'here & there a daring Humbleness of Language & Versification, and a strict adherence to matter of fact', and, as Wordsworth did not manage to resolve his doubts, he came to 'suspect that some where or other there is a radical Difference in our theoretical opinions respecting Poetry – / this I shall endeavor to go to the Bottom of'. Much of Coleridge's career as a literary thinker might be seen, in one way or another, as the protracted fulfilment of that determination, and *Biographia Literaria* is its most important production.

In the summer of 1802 Coleridge undertook an enormous solitary tour of the Lakes, filling notebooks and letters with dramatic accounts of his adventures. It was a major excursion, a hundred mile circuit of the district, Keswick to Clappersgate, Broughton Mills to St Bees, and home through Newlands, including a reckless descent from Scafell which is still famous among walkers for its daring. Relations with Sara had worsened and weren't improved by another pregnancy: 'Mrs Coleridge

Coleridge's sketch-map of the Lake District, made in the notebook he took on his expedition of 1802. Keswick and Derwentwater are in the top right-hand corner.

The British Library, Add MS 47497 f.4

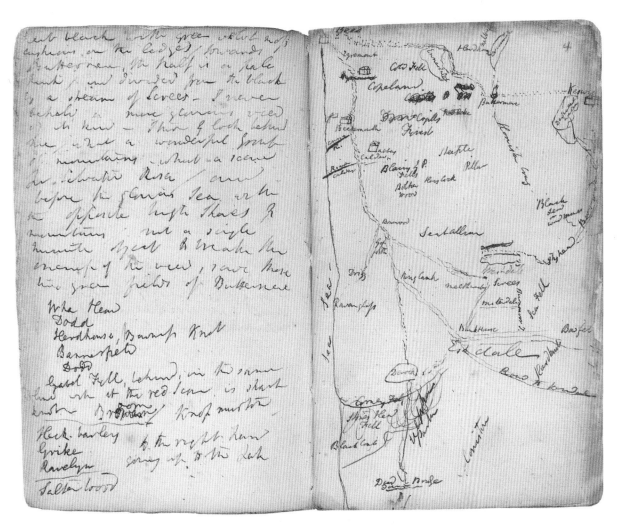

*Sir George Beaumont,
by John Wright (1812)
after John Hoppner.
Beaumont was a
generous supporter
of the painter John
Constable and of
Wordsworth and
Coleridge.*

National Portrait Gallery

… is breeding again / an event, which was to have been deprecated', he wrote, not at his most charming. In November, he left for the West Country to attend his patron Tom Wedgwood, who was protractedly dying, and they toured Wales together. On his way south Coleridge had spent a day with Sara Hutchinson, and his wife sent him an angry letter. In his reply, he reproached her jealousy, and, warming to his theme, judiciously pointed out 'that in sex, acquirements, and in the quantity and quality of natural endowments whether of Feeling, or of Intellect, you are the Inferior'. He even described their marital home as 'a mere Cat-hole', before his nerve broke: 'You know, Sally Pally! I must have a Joke – or it would not be me!' – a prospect which might have appealed to her more than he had considered.

Coleridge brought Tom Wedgwood north for a tour of the Lakes, and they arrived at Greta Hall on Christmas Eve 1802. Sara had just given birth to a daughter – also to be named Sara. 'I had never thought of a Girl as a possible event', Coleridge wrote heroically, 'however I bore the sex with great Fortitude'. She would be the most brilliant of the children, and the devoted editor of her father's works.

In the spring of the new year, Coleridge published a third edition of his poems, but his ambitions were now as much philosophical as literary. He described to Godwin a book he had 'ready to go to the Press' (it was not) which would be 'an *Instrument* of practical Reasoning in the business of real Life', comprising a history and an analysis of logic from Plato and Aristotle before setting out his own system – and all this preparatory to a yet greater work set to solve 'the two grand Problems, how, being acted upon, we shall act; how, acting, we shall be acted upon'. This is one of the first of innumerable appearances in Coleridge's letters and notebooks of the great philosophical masterwork – '*My last & great* work – always had in mind', which, continuously contemplated and never completed, would increasingly dominate his life.

In August 1803, Coleridge made an important new acquaintance. Sir George Beaumont, patron of the arts and an amateur painter himself, was travelling with his wife in the Lakes and happened to take lodgings in the back half of Greta Hall. Beaumont had met Coleridge earlier that year, and not warmed to his politics, but Coleridge charmed him in no time – 'a more amiable man with a more affectionate & kind heart does not exist', wrote Sir George, delighted, 'he is a great metaphicician [*sic*] & sometimes soars a little above my comprehension but he soon descends & is truly instructive and entertaining'. Soon Coleridge was addressing the Beaumonts as 'My dear & honored Friends!', and sending them poems – including a version of 'Dejection' which, interestingly, was addressed not to 'Sara' but to 'William'.

Shortly after that fortunate encounter, Coleridge set off with the Wordsworths on a tour of Scotland. Coleridge was fearful about his precarious health and his depressed spirits but, to judge by Dorothy's account, the trip began in a mood not so unlike the old days. They journeyed to Glasgow and then to the picturesque wonders of Loch Katrine. Shortly afterwards, they decided to part: 'poor C. being very unwell, determined to send his clothes to Edinburgh and make the best of his way thither', Dorothy wrote. Coleridge's notebook was more succinct: 'Here I left W and D … Tuesday, Aug. 30, 1803 – am to make my own way alone to Edingburgh [*sic*]'. Years later, he returned to his notebook entry,

adding: 'O Esteesee! [i.e. 'S.T.C.'] that thou hadst from thy 22nd year indeed made *thy own* way & *alone*!'.

The Wordsworths were evidently troubled by the intensity of Coleridge's feelings for Sara Hutchinson, which were obviously making everyone, including Coleridge, very unhappy. For his part, Coleridge was becoming disenchanted with what he saw as Wordsworth's egotism: 'I saw him more & more benetted in hypochondriacal Fancies, living wholly among *Devotees* – having every the minutest Thing, almost his very Eating & Drinking, done for him by his Sister, or Wife', Coleridge wrote shortly afterwards to Poole, '& I trembled, lest a Film should rise, and thicken on his moral Eye'.

After their parting, Coleridge brooded over Wordsworth's behaviour: 'My words & actions imaged on his mind, distorted & snaky as the Boatman's Oar reflected in the Lake –'. But his spirits soon restored themselves, and instead of heading to Edinburgh he set off further north on his own. He wrote to his wife two days later, 'having found myself so happy alone – such blessing is there in perfect Liberty! – that I walked off – and have walked 45 miles since then'. Following the advice of a chance acquaintance, he improvised an excursion through Glen Coe to Fort William, then to Fort Augustus and along Loch Ness to Inverness; and finally down to Perth – no mean undertaking for someone suffering with gout, but (or so he hoped) a walking cure.

The notebooks are filled with rapt accounts of things seen, massive and minute: 'on the mountain walls, for so they are, brown-green with moss, bright green with stream-hiding Grass, & pinky in streaks where the Rain-rills flowed or are flowing ... I glimpsed Trees here & there / but they looked like Apparitions'. At Fort Augustus a zealous official mistook him for a spy and he was locked up overnight, but he pressed on in the morning apparently unshaken, still absorbed by the scenery: 'Birches of all shapes & Twisture, & white Clouds of many Shapes in the blue Sky above / S[alvator] Rosa had the conifers & chesnut / I would study the Birch / it should be my only Tree'. (Salvator Rosa's paintings are celebrated for their wild scenery of forests and mountainscapes.)

He finally reached Perth on 10 September, having covered, by his own calculation, 263 miles in eight days. A letter from Southey was waiting: the Southeys'

Opposite page:

Waterfall at Keswick, watercolour by Sir George Beaumont (1803). It was while touring the Lake District in 1803 that Beaumont fortuitously encountered Coleridge at Greta.

Tate Gallery, London

*Coleridge's notebook
records his parting from
the Wordsworths during
the tour of Scotland. At
the bottom of the page:
'Tuesday, Aug. 30,
1803 – am to make my
own way alone to
Edingburgh'. Coleridge
has added later:
'O Esteesee! that thou
hadst from thy 22nd
year indeed made* thy
own *way & alone!'.*

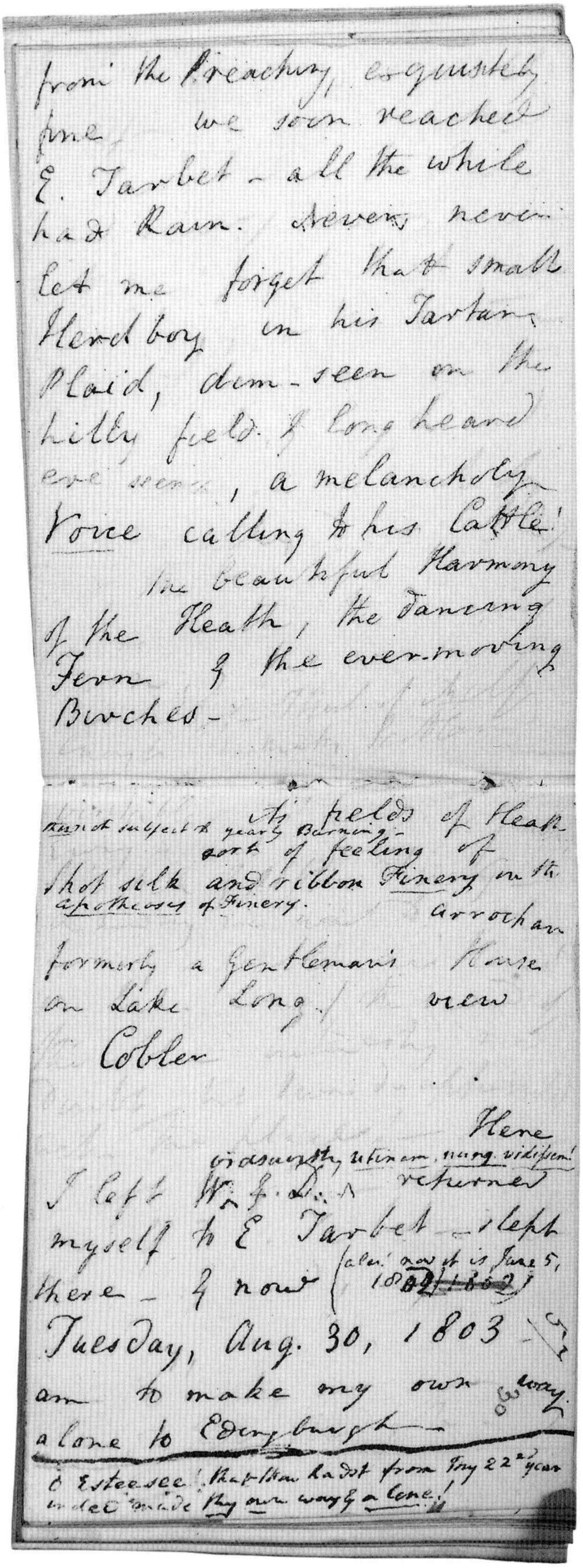

The British Library,
Add MS 47504 ff.29v–30

little girl had died, and they had moved into Greta Hall so that Edith could be with her sister. Coleridge wrote emotionally, 'I will knit myself far closer to you than I have hitherto done – & my children shall be your's till it please God to send you another'.

Back in Keswick, Coleridge's health worsened again. He was by now severely addicted to opium, and suffering in consequence from unspeakable nightmares, and, as he told Poole, 'my repeated Night-yells had made me a Nuisance in my own House'. He vividly described the night's terrible claustophobia of 'Life-stifling Fear, soul-stifling Shame' in his poem, 'The Pains of Sleep', a kind of partner-piece to the rhapsodic opiate transport of 'Kubla Khan'. 'I have been very, very ill; and have no chance of any succession of healthy Days while I remain in this Climate.' He considered which better climate he might choose to live in, finally deciding on Malta. He left his family at Greta under the trusty 'Vice-fathership' of Southey, and spent March anxiously in London waiting for a place on a ship, writing letters of emotional farewell. He stayed with Sir George Beaumont, who had his portrait painted by James Northcote. Letters from Wordsworth arrived, pleading for notes of guidance for *The Recluse*: 'I cannot say how much importance I attach to this, if it should please God that I survive you, I should reproach myself for ever in writing the work if I had neglected to procure this help'. But Coleridge did not write him any such notes. At last, news came of a place on board the *Speedwell* and Coleridge travelled to Portsmouth, where he wrote to the Wordsworths, bleakly confessing 'a wish to retire into stoniness & to stir not, or to be diffused upon the winds & have no individual Existence. But all will become better when once I can sit down, & work: when my Time is my own, I shall be myself again'. A calm delayed departure, but the *Speedwell* finally sailed on 9 April.

Coleridge painted by James Northcote (1804). Sir George Beaumont had the painting done while Coleridge was waiting in London for a passage to Malta.

Jesus College Cambridge

Landscape with
Tourists at Loch
Katrine, *by John Knox
(c. 1810s). Coleridge
and the Wordsworths
visited Loch Katrine in
the summer of 1803.
Coleridge subsequently
went on alone,
travelling north into
the Highlands.*

*National Gallery of
Scotland*

≈ *Malta 1804–1806*

Settling into his cabin, Coleridge began by drawing up a timetable of when he would read and take notes each day, and when he would learn Italian. He carried with him manuscripts of Wordsworth poems, including part of the latest version of the autobiography – 'the Poem addressed to you', as Dorothy called it. He found it difficult to concentrate: 'I have been trying to read W. Wordsworth's Poem on the Formation of his mind', he wrote in the notebook, 'but I have not been able to deliver myself up to it'. With the attentiveness he had once bestowed on landscape, Coleridge now studied the sea, and the picturesque arrangement of the ships in convoy. (The *Speedwell* was sailing in convoy with several Royal Navy warships to guard against privateers – pirate vessels that were sponsored by hostile countries to seize British merchant ships.) Once through Gibraltar – 'Now, then, I have seen Africa!' – the journey became more trying, bad weather troubled the ship and made Coleridge very sick, and then they were becalmed – 'The Sails flapped unquietly, as if restless for the Breeze, with convulsive Snatches for air, like dying Fish'. His stomach was weak and his bowels sometimes agonizing, but he still jotted down thoughts about poetry and genius; he contemplated a work called *Comforts and Consolations*; and he resolved to write to Wordsworth, passing on recent speculations about the imaginative mind for him to include in *The Recluse* – '*Ego /* its metaphysical Sublimity'. Old works haunted him strangely:

> *Hawk with ruffled Feathers resting on the Bowsprit – Now shot at & yet did not move – how fatigued – a third time it made a gyre, a short circuit, & returned again / 5 times it was thus shot at / left the Vessel / flew to another / & I heard firing, now here, now there / & nobody shot it / but probably it perished from fatigue, & the attempt to rest upon the wave! – Poor Hawk! O strange Lust of Murder in Man! – It is not cruelty / it is mere non-feeling from non-thinking.*

And thoughts of Sara Hutchinson pressed upon him too: 'always a feeling of yearning, that at times passes into Sickness of Heart'. His only companion now was his notebook.

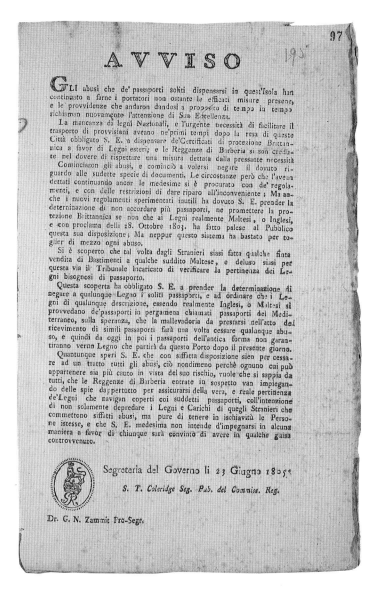

97

195

AVVISO

GLI abusi che de' passaporti soliti dispensarsi in quest'Isola han continuato a farne i portatori non ostante le efficaci misure presene, e le provvidenze che andaron dandosi a proposito di tempo in tempo richiaman nuovamente l'attenzione di Sua Eccellenza.

La mancanza di legni Nazionali, e l'urgente necessità di facilitare il trasporto di provvisioni aveano ne' primi tempi dopo la resa di queste Città obbligato S. E. a dispensare de' Certificati di protezione Brittannica a favor di Legni esteri; e le Reggenze di Barberia si son credute nel dovere di rispettare una misura dettata dalla pressante necessità.

Cominciaron gli abusi, e cominciò a volersi negare il dovuto riguardo alle sudette specie di documenti. Le circostanze però che l'aveano dettati continuando ancor le medesime si è procurato con de' regolamenti, e con delle restrizioni di dare riparo all'inconveniente; Ma anche i nuovi regolamenti sperimentati inutili ha dovuto S. E. prender la determinazione di non accordare più passaporti, ne promettere la protezione Brittannica se non che ai Legni realmente Maltesi, o Inglesi, e con proclama delli 28. Ottobre 1803. ha fatto palese al Pubblico questa sua disposizione; Ma neppur questo sistema ha bastato per togliere di mezzo ogni abuso.

Si è scoperto che tal volta dagli Stranieri siasi fatta qualche finta vendita di Bastimenti a qualche suddito Maltese, e deluso siasi per questa via il Tribunale incaricato di verificare la pertinenza dei Legni bisognosi di passaporto.

Questa scoperta ha obbligato S. E. a prender la determinazione di negare a qualunque Legno i soliti passaporti, e ad ordinare che i Legni di qualunque descrizione, essendo realmente Inglesi, o Maltesi si provvedano de' passaporti in pergamena chiamati passaporti del Mediterraneo, sulla speranza, che la mallevadoria da prestarsi nell'atto del ricevimento di simili passaporti farà una volta cessare qualunque abuso, e quindi da oggi in poi i passaporti dell'antica forma non garantiranno verun Legno che partirà da questo Porto dopo il presente giorno.

Quantunque speri S. E. che con siffatta disposizione sien per cessare ad un tratto tutti gli abusi, ciò nondimeno perchè ognuno cui può appartenere sia più cauto in vista del suo rischio, vuole che si sappia da tutti, che le Reggenze di Barberia entrate in sospetto van impiegando delle spie dappertutto per assicurarsi della vera, e reale pertinenza de' Legni che navigan coperti coi sudetti passaporti, coll'intenzione di non solamente depredare i Legni e Carichi di quegli Stranieri che commettono siffatti abusi, ma pure di tenere in ischiavitù le Persone istesse, e che S. E. medesima non intende d'impegnarsi in alcuna maniera a favor di chiunque sarà convinto di avere in qualche guisa controvvenuto.

Segreteria del Governo li 23 Giugno 1805.

S. T. Coleridge Seg. Pub. del Commiss. Reg.

Dr. G. N. Zammit Pro-Segr.

Once on Malta, Coleridge, who had not long before been taken for a possible traitor and trailed by a government agent, found himself conjured into a servant of the state. He was employed by the governor of the island, Sir Alexander Ball, as under-secretary, and subsequently as public secretary – an important post, 'the next civil dignity to the Governor', as Coleridge explained, and one which kept him 'very very busy' preparing policy papers and issuing governmental pronouncements. It was an unlikely transformation, yet he came to think of his time on Malta as 'in many respects, the most memorable and instructive period of my life'. Ball thought highly

Sir Alexander Ball, painted by Henry Pickersgill. Ball was the governor of Malta and appointed Coleridge public secretary. Coleridge came to admire him greatly and wrote a handsome tribute after his death in 1809.

National Maritime Museum, Greenwich

of Coleridge's capabilities, and grew fond of him too: 'Sir A.B. behaves to me with really personal fondness, and with almost fatherly attention', Coleridge said, evidently touched. He would later eulogise Ball as an exemplary governor, remarkable for more than his political sagacity and justice: 'the virtues of Sir Alexander Ball, as a master, a husband, and a parent, will form a no less remarkable epoch in the moral history of the Maltese than his wisdom, as a governor, has made in that of their outward circumstances'.

In August 1804, Coleridge travelled to Sicily, arriving in Syracuse in time for the opera season. The performances inspired pages of notes in the pocket notebook about metre and song, and he evidently enjoyed, as well, the company of Cecilia Bertozzi, the prima donna. His powers to charm were clearly unimpaired, and the experience 'at the bedside of the too fascinating Siren' was pleasant enough for him to feel guilty about it some years later, when he would attribute the maintenance of his virtue to a sudden vision of Sara Hutchinson's face. His thirty-second birthday arrived with a shock, recorded in his notebook: 'O Sorrow & Shame! I am not worthy to live – Two and thirty years. – & this last year above all others! – I have done nothing!' An underlying despair, about his work or his love, was always stirring: 'I am to the outward view of all cheerful, & have myself no distinct consciousness of the contrary / for I use my faculties, not indeed as once, but yet freely – but oh Sara! I am never happy, never deeply gladdened'. He sadly transcribed Shakespeare's sonnets into his notebook: 'Since I left you, mine Eye is in my mind ǀ And that which governs me to go about ǀ Doth part its function, and is partly blind, ǀ Seems seeing but effectually is out'. Really, though, Coleridge's eyes were seeing as well as ever, as the notebook testifies:

> *A Rainbow strangely preserving its form on broken clouds, with here a bit out,*
> *here a bit in, & yet still a rainbow even as you might place bits of colored*
> *ribbons at distances so as still to preserve the form of a Bow to the mind.*
> *Dec. 25. 1804*

The industry of Coleridge's public business during his time on Malta was mirrored by an intense thinking life, recorded in the private space of the notebook.

His thoughts turned memorably about imagination and poetry – including this expressive defence against charges that the poet's art is merely trivial:

> *Idly talk they who speak of Poets as mere Indulgers of Fancy, Imagination, Superstition, &c – They are the Bridlers by Delight, the Purifiers ... the true Protoplasts, Gods of Love who tame the Chaos.*

The gist of much of Coleridge's literary theory lies in the resonant phrase he uses to describe the true nobility of poets – 'Gods of Love who tame the Chaos'. Fully imaginative poets emulate the activity of God (the 'protoplast' or 'first shaper'): as God created the cosmos out of the primordial chaos of pre-existence, so the poet shapes the disorderly confusion of normal experience into the ordered worlds of art.

At the same time, Coleridge's religious thinking was reaching a kind of catastrophe. He dated one entry to the hour, half past one on 12 February 1805, as though recording an epoch in his spiritual career: 'No Christ, no God! – This I now feel with all its needful evidence, of the Understanding: would to God, my spirit were made conform thereto – that No Trinity, no God'. He was rejecting the Unitarianism which had drawn him as a young man, and accepting – or at least looking forward to accepting – the divinity of Christ. Coleridge's return to Trinitarian orthodoxy would not be complete for many years, if indeed it ever was, but from now on the shortcomings of Unitarianism (aspects of which nevertheless continued to appeal) are a recurrent feature in his writings. The shift in his views was doubtless largely due to his intensifying sense of hopelessness and his corresponding desperation to find in Christ, not merely a superlatively good man, but a divine redeemer: 'Me miserable! O yes! – Have Mercy on me, O something *out* of me!'

Terrible news reached him on the last day of March 1805. Wordsworth's brother John, a captain in the merchant fleet, had lost his ship in a storm off Portland Bill on the Dorset coast and had drowned along with many of his men. Coleridge learned of the death by chance, waiting in Sir Alexander Ball's crowded drawing room – he staggered frantically from the company gasping for breath. He had thought, as perhaps the Wordsworths had too, that John might marry Sara Hutchinson, a prospect at once agonising and yet somehow satisfactory to Coleridge. His desolation was now acute. 'Methinks, it is impossible, to live', he cried to the notebook, 'I shall hear next of Sara's Death / no, not of William's – no! no! – surely not – no surely, if there be intention in anything, or goodness in Providence'. 'Never yet has any Loss gone so far into the Life of Hope, with me', he wrote a few days later, 'I now only fear.'

He sent a letter to Grasmere, announcing his intention 'to return in the latter end of May at all events', and including some bad news of his own: 'My Ideas respecting your Recluse were burnt as a Plague-garment, and all my long letters to you and Sir George Beaumont sunk to the bottom of the Sea!' An associate, carrying many of Coleridge's papers back to England, had died of plague at Gibraltar, and his possesssions had been destroyed as a health precaution; other papers that Coleridge despatched had been lost in transit. The turmoil of these losses, on top of John's death, set him back badly, as he wrote to his wife: 'My Health *had* greatly improved; but latterly it has been very, very bad / in great measure owing to dejection of Spirits'. He was now tired of Malta, 'a barren Rock / the Sky, the Sea, the Bays, the Buildings are all

A page from a notebook Coleridge used on Malta (1804). The third entry is one of his most evocative declarations of the grandeur of poetry: 'Idly talk they who speak of Poets as mere Indulgers of Fancy…'.

The British Library, Add MS 47518 ff.117v–118

beautiful / but no rivers, no brooks, no Hedges, no green fields, almost no Trees, & the few that are are unlovely'. And he was tired, too, of his governmental duties, though he was unable to quit them until relieved. That finally happened in mid-September, when he promptly left for Sicily. 'Syracuse *again* / & again the Prima Donna', he wrote in the notebook. He had another dismal birthday of self-reproach ('O Thought of Agony! O Thought of Despair! drive me not to utter Madness!') and pondered his extinction, with the strength and fortitude of Wordsworth passionately in his thoughts: 'O that my Spirit purged by Death of its Weaknesses, which are alas! my *identity* might flow into *thine*, & live and act in thee, & be Thou'.

Coleridge arrived in Naples in November, returning after an excursion to Salerno in mid-December, and he was in Rome on New Year's Day 1806. Napoleon had just won the battle of Austerlitz, and his troops were said to be advancing on Rome: 'To stay or not to stay' Coleridge wondered in the notebook, and decided to stay. Rome had a lively international community of artists, including the German poet Ludwig Tieck and the American painter Washington Allston. Allston later recollected: 'He used to call Rome "the silent city," but I could never think of it as such while with him, for meet him when and where I would, the fountain of his mind was never dry, but, like the far-reaching aqueducts that once supplied this mistress of the world, its living stream seemed especially to flow for every classic ruin over which we wandered'. Allston sparked in Coleridge an interest in painting, and they grew very close, developing a friendship which would endure: 'to you & to you alone since I have left England', Coleridge wrote to him, 'I have felt more / and had I not known the Wordsworths, should have loved & esteemed you *first* and *most*'. They journeyed together to the picturesque mountainous landscape of Olevano, near Rome, which Coleridge thought fine – indeed almost like Keswick. He went on to visit the Sistine Chapel and attended a service at St Peter's; he travelled to Florence where he visited the Uffizi Gallery (there is so little about this visit in the surviving notebooks that it is hard not to believe some lost); and then went on to Pisa.

During all this tourism, the situation was growing increasingly desperate for any Englishmen left on the continent. Although the French fleet had been destroyed at the battle of Trafalgar, Napoleon's land forces had now won him control of most of Europe. Coleridge had hoped to return home overland to avoid another sea voyage, but that was now obviously impossible, and he eventually managed with some difficulty to secure passage on an American ship, the *Gosport*, which sailed on 23 June. The journey was as dreadful as he feared: '55 days of Ship-board, working up against head winds, rotting & sweating in calms, or running under hard gales, with the dead lights secured / & from the Captain and my fellow-passenger I received every possible Tenderness'. He had been forced to leave many of his papers behind with an acquaintance in Naples, and the captain of the *Gosport* had been forced to throw many more overboard when pursued by a 'Spanish Privateer Ruffian'. As a result, Coleridge arrived back in England with only two pocket notebooks out of all the manuscripts he had worked upon while away.

London and the Lakes 1806–1810

'I will come as soon as I can come', Coleridge wrote to Southey at Greta Hall, but he lingered in the south of England for some months, waiting for the trunk of books he had brought back from Malta to clear quarantine. He was intending to give a series of lectures on the 'Principles common to the Fine Arts' and needed the books to prepare for them, but there was another reason for delay, as Wordsworth explained sadly to Sir George Beaumont: 'he dare not go home, he recoils so much from the thought of domesticating with Mrs Coleridge, with whom, though on many accounts he much respects her, he is so miserable that he dare not encounter it'. Instead, Coleridge moved into the offices of the *Courier* newspaper, owned by Daniel

Bardon Hill from Coleorton, *by Sir George Beaumont (c.1808). A view of part of Beaumont's Leicestershire estate, where Coleridge moved to stay with the Wordsworths in 1806.*

Leicester City Museums

Stuart, his former employer on the *Morning Post*. Coleridge's letters of the time dwell upon religion, mulling over the change in his views that had occurred on Malta, away from the Unitarian optimism which had stirred the younger man and toward 'a sense of our fallen nature; and the incapability of man to heal himself'. His deeper introspection, he told Sara Coleridge's brother, was the fruit of his unhappiness: 'sorrow, and ill health, and disappointment in the only deep wish I had ever cherished, forced me to look into myself'.

On 23 October he finally headed north, not to go home, but to join the Wordsworths in the hope of catching Sara Hutchinson. Having long waited for Coleridge to materialise, Wordsworth had accepted Sir George Beaumont's offer of a farmhouse on his estate at Coleorton in Leicestershire, and Sara was due to join them as they made their way there. The Wordsworths were eager to see Coleridge again, not least for the sake of the great epic: 'He is very anxious to get forward with *The Recluse*, and is reading for the nourishment of his mind, prepatory to beginning', Dorothy had written to Lady Beaumont the previous Christmas, 'but I do not think he will be able to do much more till we have heard of Coleridge'. Coleridge had planned to seek out Sara at Penrith, where she was staying, but he arrived only to discover that she had already left to join the Wordsworth party heading south. He finally met up with them all in Kendal, on the evening of 26 October 1806. The Wordsworths were terribly dismayed: 'He is utterly changed', Dorothy wrote to a friend, 'and yet sometimes, when he was animated in conversation concerning things removed from him, I saw something of his former self'. Coleridge had gained a lot of weight and looked sick. He refused to talk about anything personal except his overwhelming desire to separate from his wife.

The unhappy Wordsworths set off to Leicestershire, and Coleridge headed for Greta Hall, arriving, after almost three years away, on 30 October. He entered the date in the notebook and underlined it, as though in dismal emphasis. A fortnight or so later, he sent a bitter letter to the Wordsworths about his wife: 'Her temper, and selfishness, her manifest dislike of me (as far as her nature is capable of a *positive* feeling) and her self-encouraged admiration of Southey as a vindictive feeling in which she delights herself as satirizing me &c. &c … We have *determined* to part absolutely and finally'. Sara Coleridge was frantic at the thought of separation, and Southey was deeply disapproving, entertaining no doubts where the blame lay. As he told a correspondent: 'His present scheme is to live with the Wordsworths – it is from his idolatry of that family that this has begun'. Wordsworth had pressed Coleridge to join them at Coleorton: 'You might bring Hartley with you, and live here as long as you liked free of all expense but washing', he wrote, in a kindly and practical spirit – better that than delivering lectures in London, anyway, where he would have to endure 'late hours and being led too much into company'. Coleridge accepted the offer, and turned up just before Christmas with Hartley in tow.

He was more passionately obsessed with Sara Hutchinson than ever: 'I know, you love me! – My reason knows it, my heart feels it … O bring my whole nature into balance and harmony'. His fraught emotions about her and about Wordsworth and his own sense of inadequacy soon created a catastrophe. On 27 December he convinced himself that he saw Wordsworth and Sara in bed together: he wrote in his notebook, in a large hand, 'The Epoch', and what he saw, or thought he saw, returned to haunt him months later – 'O the vision of that Saturday Morning – of the Bed'. Wordsworth's sexual dalliance with his sister-in-law does not seem very likely, and Coleridge himself came to think of the vision as 'a mere Phantasm', bred out of his frantic desire for Sara and his self-deploring reverence for Wordsworth, 'greater, better, manlier, more dear, by nature, to Woman, than I – I – miserable I!' Anyway, he must have kept the catastrophe to himself, perhaps not fully believing its reality even at the time. Only a few days later, he sat rapt listening to Wordsworth recite the thirteen-book version of *The Prelude*, known to the circle as the 'Poem to Coleridge', which Wordsworth had finished while its addressee had been abroad. Coleridge wrote an emotional answering poem: 'O friend! O Teacher! God's great gift to me!'. Wordsworth, able to regard life 'calm and sure | From the dread watch-tower of man's absolute Self', appears in Coleridge's lines as everything that Coleridge, listening with 'a heart forlorn', is not. As Coleridge ends his poem he finds himself in prayer, as did his Ancient Mariner.

Wordsworth noticed what seemed a permanent change in his friend, and must have begun to despair of the all-important, but still unforthcoming, notes for *The Recluse*. His sad little poem, 'A Complaint', contrasts the silent still waters of Coleridge now with the ever-flowing fountain he once had been – 'Such change, and at the very door | Of my fond heart, hath made me poor'. The company travelled together to London in April 1807, but the following month Coleridge and Hartley went on separately to Bristol, where Sara Coleridge was staying with her sister. There Coleridge made contact with Joseph Cottle again: 'you will find me the wretched wreck of what you knew me, rolling, rudderless', he warned, but Cottle was more interested in hearing his old friend argue so splendidly against the Unitarians. The Coleridges travelled on to stay with Thomas Poole in Nether Stowey, and planned a visit with Sara to the Coleridge family in Devon, so Coleridge explained, 'as a debt of respect to her for her many praiseworthy qualities' – their separation was to be a civilised one. But then Coleridge learned that his family in Ottery would not receive him, which left him angry and humiliated, and, already anxious about the likely suspension of the vital Wedgwood money, desperate and harried – 'I am to be penniless, resourceless, in heavy debt – my health & spirits absolutely broken down – & with scarce a friend in the world'.

But his spirits picked up as he prolonged his residence with the loyal Poole, and, during a stay at nearby Bridgwater, he made an interesting new acquaintance in the young Thomas De Quincey, later one of the great essayists of the age and one of the most vivid – if sometimes most scurrilous – of Coleridge's biographers. De Quincey was already an admirer and prepared to be impressed, and he found Coleridge in obliging full flow, as he recollected in an autobiographical essay written shortly after Coleridge's death:

> *He told me that there would be a very large dinner party on that day, which perhaps might be disagreeable to a perfect stranger; but, if not, he could assure me of a most hospitable welcome from the family. I was too anxious to see him under all aspects, to think of declining this invitation. And these little points of business being settled, – Coleridge, like some great river, the Orellana, or the St. Lawrence, that had been checked and fretted by rocks or thwarting islands, and suddenly recovers its volume of waters, and its mighty music, – swept at once, as if returning to his natural business, into a continuous strain of eloquent dissertation, certainly the most novel, the most finely illustrated, and traversing the most spacious fields of thought, by transitions the most just and logical, that it was possible to conceive.*

At the end of July, De Quincey escorted Sara and the children to Bristol, where Coleridge joined them in September, 'in excellent health, and improved looks', as Sara was pleased to report to Poole. But her hopes that the marriage might be back on course again soon evaporated: 'he said he must go to Town *immediately* about the Lectures'.

Despite Wordsworth's disapproval of the scheme, Coleridge had pursued the idea of a series of literary lectures at the Royal Institution, and he travelled to London in November to finalise arrangements while De Quincey took his family back up to Keswick. During December, Coleridge travelled back and forth from his lodgings in the *Courier* office to Bristol, where he stayed with his friends the Morgans: John Morgan was a friend from Coleridge's earliest Bristol days, and lived with his wife Mary and her sister Charlotte Brent. Coleridge quickly became very close to them all: 'I never knew two pairs of human beings so alike, as Mrs Morgan & her Sister, Charlotte Brent, and Mary and Sara', he told Dorothy Wordsworth, which was praise indeed. He was full of hope about his lectures on 'Poetry and the Principles of Taste', an ambitious series which would range from Ancient Greek to modern English.

The series finally began in January 1808. Coleridge would become one of the most celebrated speakers of his day, but it was a shaky start as he was ill again. He missed several lectures, and only managed to begin in earnest at the end of March, appearing twice a week thereafter to catch up. 'I am very, very busy', he wrote home to Hartley, 'and for your sake, and that of Derwent and Sara, and my Wife, your dear dear Mother'. The first lecture was somewhat abstract, but once the series resumed he began to improve, and by the third he told his audience that his mind had 'gradually regained its buoyancy'. It certainly had. The lectures he gave in the spring of 1808 are the first public sighting of Coleridge the critic of Shakespeare: his eminence as a Shakespearean critic is only rivalled by his predecessor Samuel Johnson. Coleridge approached Shakespeare in the lectures by analysing the different faculties brought into concert in *Venus and Adonis* – including the 'Love of Natural Objects', 'Fancy, or the aggregative Power', and, pre-eminently, 'Imagination', that faculty which draws diverse images and ideas together, 'combining many circumstances into one moment of thought to produce that ultimate end of human Thought, and human Feeling, Unity'. Coleridge spoke, too, about the 'profound, energetic & philosophical mind' which was implicit in Shakespeare's poetry, emphasising a belief which he had long held – that 'No man was ever yet a great poet, without being at the same time a profound philosopher'.

Wordsworth, who was visiting London, heard one of the lectures and had to concede that Coleridge 'seemed to give great satisfaction'. Henry Crabb Robinson, a barrister and keen man of letters, attended many of the series and wrote about them with less reserve, repeating Coleridge's best remarks and evoking the winning eccentricity of his performance – 'Coleridge's digressions are not the worst parts of his lectures, or rather he is always digressing'. The diary of Joseph Farington, a leading figure in the Royal Academy, records a moment which implies Coleridge's instinctive command of platform theatricality:

> *When Coleridge came into the Box there were several Books laying. He opened two or three of them silently and shut them again after a short inspection. He then paused, & leaned His head on His hand, and at last said, He had been thinking for a word to express the distinct character of Milton as a Poet, but not finding one that w[oul]d express it, He should make one – 'Ideality.' He spoke extempore.*

Coleridge's improvisational skills became famous. He began one lecture with an apology for having lost his notes on the way to the theatre, but nevertheless, according to De Quincey who was attending, he 'managed to get through very well'. At another lecture, he had a disturbing encounter with his past when his first love, Mary Evans, now Mary Todd, introduced herself. He was shocked to find her marriage more wretched even than his own – 'a counterpart of the very worst parts of my own Fate, in an exaggerated Form'.

By June he had had enough, and withdrew from the rest of his series. In September, he was back in the Lakes again, staying with the Wordsworths who had now returned to Grasmere and moved into a substantial house at the north end of the village called Allan Bank. 'Re-arrived at Grasmere and entered the new House for the first time', Coleridge recorded in the notebook. The Wordsworths had originally taken the house with thoughts of Coleridge's residence in mind, but, as Dorothy explained to a friend, they had subsequently wondered whether it were 'prudent for us to consent to it, C. having been so very unsteady in all things since his return to England'. Since then, confirming such anxieties, there had been a difficult exchange with Wordsworth, whom Coleridge had wildly accused of reading his letters to Sara Hutchinson: 'She is 34 years of age', Wordsworth protested, 'and what have I to do with overlooking her letters!' But if the exchange did not bode well, it was evidently put out of mind, and Coleridge was welcomed to Allan Bank warmly. With him came his daughter Sara, who could scarcely have known her father: 'Every one is delighted with her', Coleridge wrote back reassuringly to her mother, 'indeed, it is absolutely impossible that there can be a sweeter or a sweetlier behaved Child'.

Coleridge had a new project in hand. This was a periodical, which he considered calling *The Upholder* but finally named *The Friend*, a firmly highbrow enterprise which was to provide for the minority tastes of the intelligentsia. 'I do not write in this Work for the *Multitude*', Coleridge told Humphry Davy, 'but for those, who by Rank, or Fortune, or official Situation, or Talents and Habits of Reflection, are to *influence* the Multitude'. Wordsworth entertained no expectations of success: 'It is I think too clear that Coleridge is not sufficiently master of his own efforts to execute anything which requires a regular course of application to one object'. The 'Prospectus' that Coleridge issued certainly struck an unlikely note: 'I have not only planned, but collected the Materials for, many Works on various and important Subjects: so many indeed, that the Number of my unrealized Schemes, and the Mass of my miscellaneous Fragments, have often furnished my Friends with a Subject of Raillery, and sometimes of Regret and Reproof'. The new journal was to gather together such unpromising-sounding fragments – which certainly made an ingenuous sales-pitch.

Coleridge worked hard at the launch over the winter and spring, and placed advertisements for a periodical 'to uphold those Truths and those Merits, which are founded in the nobler and permanent parts of our Nature against the Caprices of Fashion'. The first number of *The Friend* belatedly appeared in June. Wordsworth's response was gloomy: 'I am sorry for it – as I have not the least hope that it can proceed', but Dorothy, perhaps to her surprise, recognised Coleridge's 'good spirits'

Following pages:

Grasmere and Helm Crag, *a watercolour by Peter de Wint (c.1821). Coleridge returned to the Lakes in September 1808 and joined the Wordsworths at Allan Bank, to the north of the village.*

Victoria and Albert Museum

Title page of The Friend, *'A Literary, Moral, and Political Weekly Paper …' published by Coleridge from Grasmere. Its aim was unashamedly highbrow: 'to uphold those Truths and those Merits, which are founded in the nobler and permanent Parts of our Nature'.*

The British Library, C126.K.8

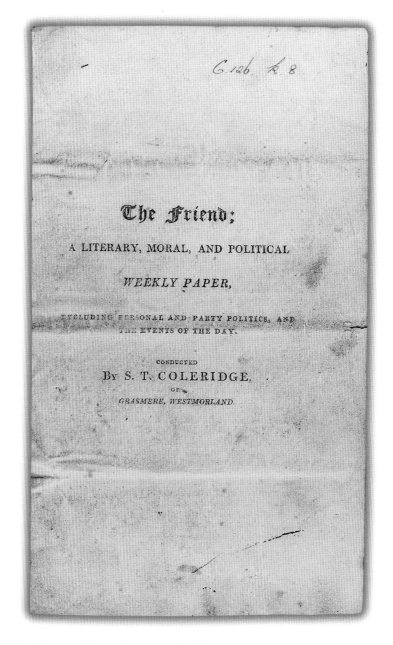

and admired his tenacity: 'what human body but one of extraordinary strength could have stood out against the trials which he has put his to?' From the fourth number, Sara Hutchinson acted as Coleridge's collaborator, taking down essays from his dictation, and they obviously worked together well. There were some problems with the paper supply which delayed a few early issues, but otherwise the weekly instalments appeared more or less on time until the twenty-seventh, on 15 March 1810.

Coleridge launched off in an expansively abstract cast of mind, with a discussion of the freedom of the press that extended over several issues. Dorothy Wordsworth was not alone in thinking the first number 'certainly obscure', but later numbers were more approachable, including a vivid portrait of Luther (one of Coleridge's heroes), some reworkings of his letters from Germany, and an account of the life of Sir Alexander Ball. Southey and Wordsworth contributed too. *The Friend* also published poems, Coleridge's own and Wordsworth's, including the first appearance in print of fragments from *The Prelude*. The productivity was remarkable and fitfully intense, an entire number sometimes written in a couple of days: 'he either does a great deal or nothing at all', Dorothy marvelled.

The complete run remains a brilliant, eccentric miscellany, but it was not designed to be popular, and Coleridge was soon fretting to Southey 'that the plan and execution of *The Friend* is so utterly unsuitable to the public taste as to preclude all rational hopes of its success'. Subscription arrangements had been badly mishandled, so money was always a problem, and running the journal proved more than mentally draining. There was no direct post between Grasmere and Penrith, where *The Friend* was printed, and Coleridge had several times to make the arduous journey on foot by the Kirkstone Pass. In the end, there was an additional reason for publication to lapse: Sara Hutchinson was growing weary, too, and on 5 March left Grasmere to stay with her brother. 'Coleridge most of all will miss her', Dorothy predicted, 'as she has transcribed almost every Paper of the Friend for the press', but Dorothy thought the enterprise doomed anyway: 'He was tired, and she had at last no power to drive him on'. A month after the last number, Coleridge was still speaking of *The Friend* as a current concern, and the Wordsworths were despairing. 'We have no hope of him', wrote Dorothy, 'He will tell me that he has been writing, that he has written half a Friend; when I know that he has not written a single line'. Coleridge retreated to his room, confessing to 'a depression of spirits, little less than absolute Despondency'. His feelings for Sara Hutchinson were as troubling as ever, even though Dorothy briskly dismissed them as 'no more than a fanciful dream'.

Coleridge returned to Greta Hall in May, ostensibly to discuss Hartley's future, but he ended up staying the whole summer – 'and in all that time he has not *appeared* to be employed in composition', as Sara Coleridge wrote anxiously to Poole, 'although he has repeatedly assured me he was'. He was strong enough to instruct his wife and daughter in Italian, but his health was a cause of concern. An acquaintance, Basil Montagu, urged him to undergo medical treatment for his opium addiction in London, where he could lodge with the Montagus, and Coleridge agreed. Wordsworth, who was sadly expert in the subject, felt himself obliged to warn Montagu about Coleridge's habits as a houseguest. Once Coleridge was in London, Montagu, for some inexplicable reason, thought to tell Coleridge what (he claimed) Wordsworth had said – that 'he has no Hope of you', that 'for years past [you] had been an ABSOLUTE NUISANCE in the Family', that Coleridge had habitually run up debts 'at little Pot-Houses for Gin', and indeed that he was a *'rotten drunkard'* who was 'rotting out his entrails by intemperance'. Coleridge was bewildered and devastated, and poured out his grief to the notebook: 'No Hope of me! absol[ute] Nuisance! God's mercy is it a Dream! … Whirled about without a center – as in a nightmair – no gravity – a vortex without a center'.

The poets did not communicate for a year and a half. A kind of reconciliation was eventually patched together, but anything like the old intimacy was lost for ever. Coleridge would never live with the Wordsworths, nor settle in the Lakes, again. On his very last visit, in February 1812, he rode through Grasmere without stopping. 'Poor Hartley sat in speachless [*sic*] astonishment as the Chaise passed the turning to the Vicarage where W. lives, but he dared not hazard one remark', Sara told Poole, 'and Derwent fixed his eyes full of tears upon his father, who turned his head away to conceal his own emotions'.

~ *Man of Letters 1810–1816*

S tunned by Montagu's disclosure, Coleridge looked for somewhere in London to stay. The plan to move in with the Montagus was obviously impossible now. He stayed for some days in a hotel in Covent Garden where he wrote passionately in a notebook about his religious faith and, inextricably entwined with it, his desperate, overpowering feelings for Sara Hutchinson: 'To bid me not love you were to bid me annihilate myself … you are the God within me'. He also spent several pages analysing his own character, lamenting the unkindnesses he felt he had suffered from Wordsworth while he identified the weakness in himself that seemed to invite them: 'My habitual abasement of myself & talents in comparison with the merits of my Friend'.

Coleridge's old Bristol friends, the Morgans, were now living in Hammersmith and he moved in with them. He later described them to Wordsworth as his 'Saviours, Body and Soul', explaining with unforgiving self-analysis: 'my moral Will was, & I fear is, so weakened relatively to my Duties to myself, that I cannot act, as I ought to do, except under the influencing knowle[d]ge of it's effects on those I love & believe myself loved by'. Within his new family, he now started piecing together his London life. Over the next few months he began writing for the *Courier* and socialised; and, of course, he talked. The diary of Henry Crabb Robinson records several sightings (and hearings) of Coleridge at literary dinners: 'Coleridge … talked a vast deal, and delighted every one'. Not everyone was so tolerant of his holding forth though: Madame de Staël, the celebrated author of *Corinne* and no mean talker herself, complained, 'He is very great in monologue, but he has no idea of dialogue'. But most of his listeners seem to have been too struck to object. Coleridge paid a visit to his nephews, the sons of his brother James, in the spring of 1811, and his conversation struck them as droll as well as brilliant, ranging from German metaphysics and contemporary politics to Milton's poetry and the genius of Aristotle – 'so delightful and astonishing a man I have never met with', one reported.

Coleridge's abilities were apparently undiminished, but the break with Wordsworth secretly festered – 'so deep and so rankling is the wound, which

Wordsworth has wantonly and without the slightest provocation inflicted in return for a 15 years' most enthusiastic, self-despising & alas! self-injuring Friendship'. In October he left the Morgans following some confrontation about his drug-taking, and took lodgings in the Strand. 'Coleridge has powdered his head, and looks like Bacchus, Bacchus ever sleek and young', a delighted Lamb reported to the Wordsworths, 'He is going to turn sober, but his Clock has not struck yet, meantime he pours down goblet after goblet, the 2[n]d to see where the 1st is gone, the 3[r]d to see no harm happens to the second, a fourth to say there's another coming, and a 5th to say he's not sure he's the last'.

He now returned to the lecture theatre, announcing a course of lectures on Shakespeare and Milton 'in Illustration of the Principles of Poetry'. He delivered the lectures in Scot's Corporation Hall off Fleet Street, twice weekly, from November to the following January, despite his fragile health. This series was an immense success. Regularly reported in the press, it became part of the London scene, attended by celebrities like Byron and the poet Samuel Rogers, and the novelist Mary Russell Mitford, who left (she said) feeling 'quite Coleridgified'. His manner had not grown any less digressive, as Henry Crabb Robinson noted: 'He began with identifying religion with love, delivered a rhapsody on brotherly and sisterly love, which seduced him into a dissertation on incest. I at last lost all power of attending to him'. But practised auditors could be more understanding, as Crabb Robinson also reported: 'when Coleridge was running from topic to topic, Lamb said, "This is not much amiss. He promised a lecture on the Nurse in 'Romeo and Juliet,' and in its place he has given us one in the *manner* of the Nurse"'.

Making records of Coleridge's lectures was extremely difficult, but the shorthandist John Payne Collier attended this series and made remarkably full transcriptions of what Coleridge said. He published his account of the lectures in 1856 as *Seven Lectures on Shakespeare and Milton by the late S.T. Coleridge*, a book in part responsible for establishing Coleridge's reputation as one of the greatest of English critics. In these lectures, Coleridge discussed the idea of taste, the definition of poetry, and the different species of readers; he described Shakespeare's genius and returned to *Venus and Adonis* as evidence of it; he distinguished between the empathetic power of Shakespeare ('darting himself forth, and passing himself into all

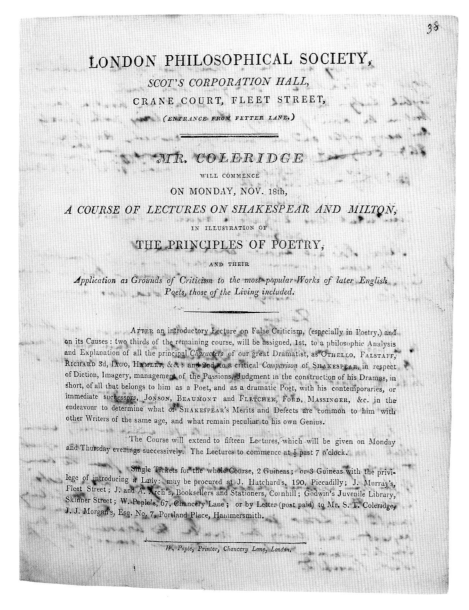

38

LONDON PHILOSOPHICAL SOCIETY,

SCOT'S CORPORATION HALL,

CRANE COURT, FLEET STREET,

(ENTRANCE FROM FETTER LANE.)

MR. COLERIDGE

WILL COMMENCE

ON MONDAY, NOV. 18th,

A COURSE OF LECTURES ON SHAKESPEAR AND MILTON,

IN ILLUSTRATION OF

THE PRINCIPLES OF POETRY,

AND THEIR

Application as Grounds of Criticism to the most popular Works of later English Poets, those of the Living included.

AFTER an introductory Lecture on False Criticism, (especially in Poetry,) and on its Causes: two thirds of the remaining course, will be assigned, 1st, to a philosophic Analysis and Explanation of all the principal *Characters* of our great Dramatist, as OTHELLO, FALSTAFF, RICHARD 3d, IAGO, HAMLET, &c. and 2nd, to a critical *Comparison* of SHAKESPEAR, in respect of Diction, Imagery, management of the Passions, Judgment in the construction of his Dramas, in short, of all that belongs to him as a Poet, and as a dramatic Poet, with his contemporaries, or immediate successors, JONSON, BEAUMONT and FLETCHER, FORD, MASSINGER, &c. in the endeavour to determine what of SHAKESPEAR's Merits and Defects are common to him with other Writers of the same age, and what remain peculiar to his own Genius.

The Course will extend to fifteen Lectures, which will be given on Monday and Thursday evenings successively. The Lectures to commence at ½ past 7 o'clock.

Single Tickets for the whole Course, 2 Guineas; or 3 Guineas with the privilege of introducing a Lady: may be procured at J. Hatchard's, 190, Piccadilly; J. Murray's, Fleet Street; J. and A. Arch's, Booksellers and Stationers, Cornhill; Godwin's Juvenile Library, Skinner Street; W. Pople's, 67, Chancery Lane; or by Letter (post paid) to Mr. S. T. Coleridge, J. J. Morgan's, Esq. No. 7, Portland Place, Hammersmith.

W. Pople, Printer, Chancery Lane, London.

Prospectus for Coleridge's very successful twice-weekly series of lectures 'on Shakespear and Milton, in illustration of the Principles of Poetry'.

The British Library, Add MS 34225 f.38

the forms of human character & human passion') and the sublime egotism of Milton (who 'attracted all forms & all things to himself into the unity of his own grand ideal'); and he analysed the structure and characterisation of several individual Shakespeare plays, including *Romeo and Juliet*, *The Tempest*, and *Hamlet*. Coleridge's close reading is always eye-opening, as in his fine praise for Prospero's words to Miranda in *The Tempest*, 'hurried thence | Me and thy crying self' – 'by introducing the simple happy epithet *crying* in the last line', says Coleridge, 'a complete picture

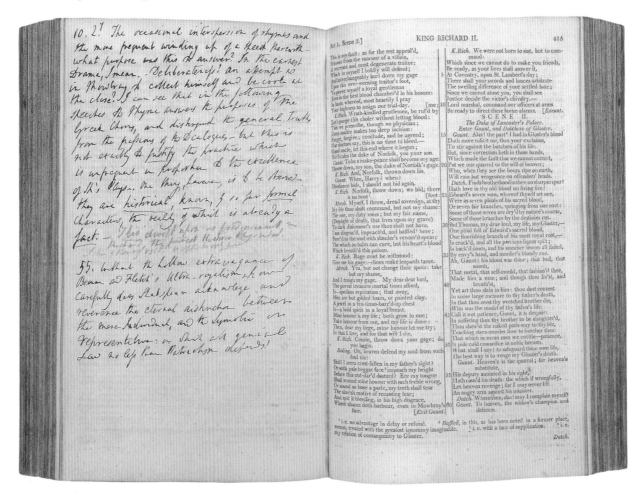

is present to the mind'. The quickness of his appreciation makes itself felt in the exuberance of his similes – 'The Wit of Shakespeare was like the flourishing of a man's stick when he is walking along in the full flow of animal spirits' – and the marvellous fineness of his psychological observation – 'there is an effort in the mind when it would describe what it cannot satisfy itself with the description of, to reconcile opposites and to leave a middle state of mind … when it is hovering between two images'. The account of Prince Hamlet, especially, was to become one of his most celebrated contributions to Shakespearean criticism: 'a person in whose view the external world and all its incidents and objects were comparatively dim, and of no interest in themselves, and which began to interest only when they were reflected in the mirror of his mind'. Someone whispered to Crabb Robinson that that sounded like a self-critical satire: 'No', Crabb Robinson replied, 'it is an Elegy'.

Coleridge had found a form ideally suited to his extemporising genius, and he gave two more sets of lectures later in the year, about European drama from the Greeks and about Shakespeare again. Wordsworth was in town and attended some of them, and felt bound to admit that lecturing was 'upon the whole quite eligible for him'. (It was during this time that Lamb and Crabb Robinson worked to reconcile the two poets.) Another series of lectures, on 'Belles Lettres', followed in the winter and ran through to January 1813. Upon entering the room for the last one, Crabb Robinson reported, Coleridge 'was received with three rounds of applause … and very loudly applauded during the lecture and at its close'. The depressive listlessness which had followed on the failure of *The Friend* was now quite vanished. He reissued *The Friend* in a new edition in June 1812; he published *Omniana*, an anthology of *aperçus* and anecdotes co-authored with Southey; and his old tragedy *Osorio*, now entitled *Remorse*, was accepted by the Drury Lane Theatre. There it played for twenty performances in January 1813, a good run, and it was very well received – '*unexampled* APPLAUSE', Coleridge wrote home proudly. When he made an appearance in the theatre he was loudly cheered. The play was printed and quickly went through three editions.

The Surrey Institution, by T. Rowlandson and C.A. Pugin (c.1810), showing a lecture in progress. Coleridge gave his series of lectures on 'belles lettres' at the institution in the winter of 1812–13.

The British Museum, 1586–7–12–765

Coleridge engraved after a portrait by George Dawe (1811–12). Coleridge thought Dawe's drawing a very good likeness, only surpassed by a portrait done by Washington Allston in Rome in 1806.

The British Library, 10825 e.25

Coleridge had made things up with the Morgans and moved back in with them in the spring of 1812. But disaster struck in August 1813, when Morgan suddenly went bankrupt and fled to Ireland. Coleridge rushed to help. He pawned many of his books and arranged to let the London house, and he relocated himself to the Morgans' hometown of Bristol to attend to creditors. He gave more lectures on Shakespeare and a new series on education. He settled Mary and Charlotte at Ashley, near Box, in Wiltshire, and there Morgan shortly joined them. Coleridge's activity was hectic, and in December his health broke. He lay badly sick for several desperate days in a hotel room in Bath, and wrote desperately to a Baptist minister acquaintance, 'O God save me – save me from myself'. He eventually made it back to Bristol, where he stayed with Josiah Wade, an old friend from *Watchman* days. Yet more lectures were announced for January, on Milton and Cervantes, but the state of his health meant they had to be delayed until the spring. Wade looked after him devotedly, and Coleridge began to improve again. He renewed his acquaintance with Allston, who was living in Bristol: Allston painted his portrait, a fine portrait (see page 104) showing a dignified, grey-haired figure. Allston was pleased with it, but Coleridge bemoaned his 'FEEBLE, unmanly face'.

In September 1814, Coleridge joined the Morgans, first at Ashley, and then at Calne, in Wiltshire, where he moved with them at the end of the year. It was a hopeful time: Hartley's future seemed sorted out, with a place at Merton College, Oxford, and Coleridge himself was back in the midst of a surrogate family. He enjoyed Calne's society, and his morale rose. He began to plan an immense work, an analysis and synthesis of all preceding philosophy which would demonstrate 'that Christianity is true Philosophy, & of course that all true Philosophy is Christianity'.

This would be 'the Work, on which I would wish to ground my reputation with Posterity, if I should have any', as he explained to his old editor Daniel Stuart, 'It's Title will be Logosophia, or on the Logos human & Divine, in six Treatises'. (The 'Logos' is Christ, the incarnated 'Word' of the first verse of St. John's Gospel: 'In the beginning was the Word'.) The 'Logosophia' – and other versions of the great work under different names – would dominate the last two decades of Coleridge's intellectual life. It was an unfinishable masterwork that would articulate his comprehensive system of philosophy, and, as he put it in later life, 'reduce all knowledges into harmony' – 'my great Work', as he said in 1820, 'to the preparation of which more than twenty years of my life have been devoted, and on which my hopes of extensive and permanent Utility, of Fame in the noblest sense of the word, mainly rest'.

He had some less speculative literary tasks in hand too. He wrote *Zapolya*, a 'dramatic Entertainment' in loose imitation of Shakespeare's *Winter's Tale*, and he gathered his poems in a volume entitled *Sibylline Leaves* (published in 1817) which contained, he said, 'all the Poems, I think worthy of publication'. He took the opportunity of the new collection to revise many of the poems, some extensively – including 'The Ancient Mariner', which now acquired its famous and sometimes perplexing marginal glosses. (For example: 'The curse is finally expiated' says the note at the side of the page – but is the Mariner's curse ever really *expiated*?) He also dictated large amounts of prose to Morgan, originally meant for an introduction to *Sibylline Leaves*, but this soon acquired a life of its own and eventually became *Biographia Literaria, or Biographical Sketches of my Literary Life and Opinions*, which, after several snags, was finally published in two volumes in 1817.

Biographia Literaria ('Literary Life') is the greatest of all the Coleridgean prose miscellanies, one of the most brilliant and among the most influential books of literary criticism in English. It is not a coherent monograph, but rather a ragbag, as full of digressions as were Coleridge's lectures. This is partly because, at the last minute, Coleridge had to fill up a large gap in volume two with what he had to hand, which included a reworking of his account of travelling to Germany in 1798. Those pages are frankly miscellaneous, but the rest of the book also proceeds in an apparently wayward manner, finding room for (among other things) a rebuttal of the

Washington Allston's portrait of Coleridge, painted in Bristol in 1814. Coleridge's daughter later called this portrait 'the best that has been taken of my Father', and Wordsworth thought it 'the only likeness of the great original that ever gave me the least pleasure'.

National Portrait Gallery

supposed irritability of men of genius, some good advice to young people tempted to take up literature as a trade – which was, *DON'T* – and a survey of the practice of contemporary reviewers. But despite this perplexing mixture, a number of recurring themes tie the book together – pre-eminently, the nature of imagination, its role in normal consciousness and its special role in the making of poetry.

As its name suggests, *Biographia* is partly an autobiography, tracing the growth of Coleridge's mind from schooldays, when his youthful immersion in metaphysics was appeased by the redemptive discovery of Bowles's sonnets, and on to the yet greater discovery of Wordsworth's poetry: 'seldom, if ever, was the emergence of an original poetic genius above the literary horizon more evidently announced'. This is the turning point in Coleridge's life history, as he presents it, for Wordsworth arrives in the story as an archetypal poetic genius. Wordsworth possesses 'the original gift of spreading the tone, the *atmosphere*, and with it the depth and height of the ideal world around forms, incidents, and situations, of which, for the common view, custom had bedimmed all the lustre, had dried up the sparkle and the dew drops'.

After this carefully dramatised moment of revelation, the rest of volume one turns to Coleridge's philosophical development, arguing at length against his youthful enthusiasms, Priestley and Hartley and other British thinkers who portrayed the mind as passive, and making common cause instead with Immanuel Kant and the German idealists for whom consciousness was, rather, intrinsically *creative*. But Coleridge is only a few chapters into his metaphysical argument when he breaks off, and prints a letter which – so he claims – he has just received from a friend, comically protesting that Coleridge leave such obscure concerns for his masterwork and cut to the main point. Really, of course, the letter was written by Coleridge himself. So, rather than a long philosophical discussion, Coleridge offers us merely his summary definition of the imagination, in what is perhaps the most famous passage of literary theory in English:

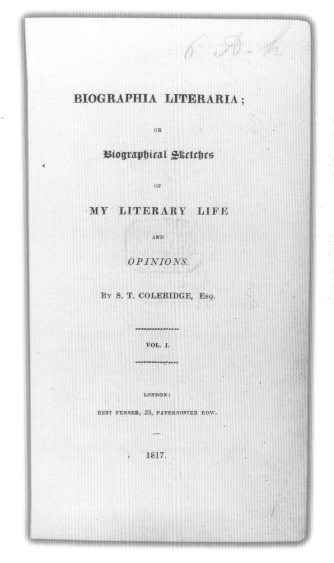

Title page of Biographia Literaria *(1817), Coleridge's seminal, unclassifiable prose work, which mixes autobiography, criticism, theology, philosophy, and reflections on the literary life, and which contains his most extensive discussion of Wordsworth's poetry.*

The British Library, 1163.c.4

> *The primary* IMAGINATION *I hold to be the living Power and prime Agent of all human Perception, and as a repetition in the finite mind of the eternal act of creation in the infinite I* AM. *The secondary I consider as an echo of the former, co-existing with the conscious will, yet still as identical with the primary in the* kind *of its agency, and differing only in* degree, *and in the* mode *of its operation. It dissolves, diffuses, dissipates, in order to re-create; or where this process is rendered impossible, yet still at all events it struggles to idealize and to unify. It is essentially* vital, *even as all objects (as* objects) *are essentially fixed and dead.*

It is a complex but immensely resonant passage, which joins together Coleridge's philosophical argument about the mind in general with his Wordsworth-centered argument about the poet's special mind in particular. The 'primary' imagination here is the innate, pre-conscious creativity that lies within all our acts of normal perception, made, as we are, in the image of God – and, in words from a Coleridge letter previously quoted, 'that too in the sublimest sense – the Image of the *Creator*'. (God is 'the infinite I AM', a Biblical phrase which Coleridge took from Exodus.) The 'secondary' imagination, used by poets (like Wordsworth), is just like the primary in the way it operates – only it is not pre-conscious, but closely involved with the poet's will (his will to write a poem). Coleridge had long entertained such ideas, in rather different language. On Malta, as we saw, he had come marvellously to think of poets as 'Gods of love that tame the chaos', which is much what he is saying in the famous paragraph from *Biographia* too. And in 'Dejection', he had discovered that objects in themselves are dead unless vitalised by the imagination's light – 'I may not hope from outward forms to win | The passion and the life, whose fountains are within'.

The bulk of Coleridge's second volume of *Biographia* then turns to Wordsworth's poetry – but this time to describe not only the way it properly fulfils the duties of the imagination, 'THE VISION AND THE FACULTY DIVINE', but also the ways in which, at other moments, it fails to. Here Coleridge drew on the sense of 'radical Difference' of which (as we have seen) he was already aware as far back as 1802. Wordsworth was strangely drawn, as it seemed, to stoop to '*a matter-of-factness … a laborious minuteness and fidelity in the representation of objects*' – at such moments, his imagination founders, his evocation of an 'ideal world' fails, and his poetry sinks to the level of the merely prosaic and ordinary. Wordsworth's highly idiosyncratic mixture of visionary power and matter-of-factness characteristically created what Coleridge saw as an 'incongruity' in the style of his poetry, and in *Biographia* Coleridge sometimes sounds very sharp about it – his hurt feelings about the Montagu affair were obviously still raw. Wordsworth was understandably wounded. But Coleridge also made what was, at the time, an extraordinarily lofty claim about his former collaborator: 'in imaginative power, he stands nearest of all modern writers to Shakespeare and Milton; and yet in a kind perfectly unborrowed and his own'.

Coleridge returned to London in March 1816, and submitted his play *Zapolya* to the Covent Garden Theatre, which promptly rejected it. His new lodgings were above a chemist's shop, the unsuitability of which for an unreformed opium addict was not lost on Charles Lamb, who reflected with amused concern that you might as well send a bookworm to recuperate at the Vatican. And Coleridge's health did indeed take another turn for the worse. He sent for John Morgan, who engaged a physician friend, one Joseph Adams, to remain at Coleridge's bedside almost constantly. By 10 April, Coleridge had recovered sufficiently to write to Byron, who, hearing of his financial troubles, generously sent him £100. Coleridge described with unnerving frankness his 'daily habit of taking enormous doses of Laudanum', but said that he was now looking forward to a life without 'the direful practice'. Despite his protestations of ill health and incapacity, Coleridge presented himself at Byron's London house within a few days, and the old magic was evidently quite undiminished. He recited his still-unpublished 'Kubla Khan', to Byron's amazement: Leigh Hunt saw Byron 'coming away from him, highly struck with his poem, and saying how wonderfully he talked' – but then, as Hunt added, '[t]his was the impression of everyone who heard him'. Lamb had heard him reciting 'Kubla Khan' too: 'it irradiates & brings heaven & Elysian bowers into my parlour while he sings or says it', he told Wordsworth, 'I think his essentials not touched, he is very bad, but then he wonderfully picks up another day, and his face when he repeats his verses hath its ancient glory, an Arch angel a little damaged'.

Title page of Coleridge's
Christabel *volume,
published at Byron's
instigation in 1816. It
was the first appearance
in print of 'Kubla
Khan' and 'The Pains
of Sleep', as well as the
unfinished poem
'Christabel'.*

*The British Library,
11642 bbb 47*

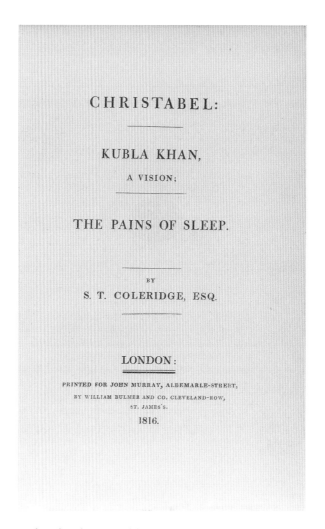

CHRISTABEL:

KUBLA KHAN,

A VISION;

THE PAINS OF SLEEP.

BY

S. T. COLERIDGE, ESQ.

LONDON:

PRINTED FOR JOHN MURRAY, ALBEMARLE-STREET,
BY WILLIAM BULMER AND CO. CLEVELAND-ROW,
ST. JAMES'S.
1816.

Byron urged Coleridge to publish the poem, and pressed the idea on his own publisher Murray. A volume duly appeared, with 'Kubla Khan' printed alongside 'The Pains of Sleep', Coleridge's opium nightmare poem, and 'Christabel', which had lain unfinished in manuscript since 1802. He received £80 for the book, which he promptly handed over to Morgan. He later claimed the publication was 'utterly against my feelings and my Judgement', done solely to raise money for his friends, but there is no mistaking the buoyancy in his correspondence at the time: 'My Health is evidently progressive; and my mind & spirits daily more easy, and tranquil'.

⟋⟍ *Sage of Highgate 1816–1834*

Coleridge's improved hopes were partly due to the prospect of a new medical regime – indeed, of a new life. In April 1816, as Coleridge began to convalesce, Joseph Adams contacted Dr James Gillman of Highgate, north London – 'a respectable Surgeon and Naturalist', as Coleridge described him to Byron. '[H]e wishes to fix himself in the house of some medical gentleman, who will have courage to refuse him any laudanum', Adams wrote to Gillman: 'As he is desirous of retirement, and a garden, I could think of no one so readily as yourself … His communicative temper will make his society very interesting, as well as useful'.

Dr James Gillman, engraved from a portrait made by C.R. Leslie in 1816, the year Coleridge moved into the Gillmans' Highgate home.

The British Library, 10825.e.25

He was right: Gillman later wrote of his first meeting with Coleridge, 'his manner, his appearance, and above all, his conversation were captivating ... I felt indeed almost spell-bound, without the desire of release'. Coleridge frankly described his enslavement to opium, and repeated some verses he had written on the subject (although Gillman didn't name these, they are presumably 'The Pains of Sleep'): Gillman was moved by his despondency, as well as struck by his powers; and Coleridge, in turn, was much taken by Gillman's kindliness. 'The first half hour, I was with you', he wrote to Gillman afterwards, 'convinced me that I should owe my reception into your family exclusively to motives not less flattering to me than honorable to yourself ... if I could not be comfortable in your House & with your family, I should deserve to be miserable'. Gillman was married, with two sons, and it is characteristic that Coleridge should have emphasised from the start, not just Gillman's medical supervision, but a place within a family. Gillman had no intention of 'receiving an inmate into my house', but what had been planned as a month's recuperation quickly became a permanent arrangement, and Coleridge was to stay with his new family for the last eighteen years of his life. He wrote to his old friend Daniel Stuart, 'You will like Mr Gillman – he is a man of strong, fervid and agile Intellect ... And his Wife it will be impossible not to respect if a Balance and Harmony of Powers and Qualities unified and spiritualized by a native feminine Fineness of Character render Womanhood amiable & respectable ... Mr Gillman as Friend and as Physician will succeed in restoring me to my natural Self'.

Coleridge's health began to improve at once, and in June, only a few weeks after arriving at the Gillmans', Coleridge had never looked so well thought Crabb Robinson, an improvement that he attributed to 'abstinence from laudanum, &c.'. Sharper-eyed Lamb regarded the set-up less confidently: 'He is at present under the medical care of a Mr Gilman (Killman?) a Highgate Apothecary', he wrote mischievously to Wordsworth, 'where he plays at leaving off Laud–m'. Lamb's suspicions were, it seems, quite accurate. Coleridge managed to procure supplies from a local chemist, but Gillman's watchful care nevertheless brought the habit under control, and Coleridge entered a new period of great productivity.

Current affairs were still preoccupying and Coleridge set to work on three *Lay Sermons* addressing 'the present Distresses' – the economic and social crisis that

Coleridge, an engraving after a portrait drawn by C.R. Leslie in 1818, when Coleridge was living in Highgate, then still a village north of London.

The British Library, 1430.c.11 vol. 2

had followed upon Britain's long-awaited defeat of Napoleon. Two sermons were published, in 1816 and 1817, addressed respectively to the higher and middle classes, designed to show 'The Bible the Best Guide to Political Skill and Foresight'. The first sermon idiosyncratically interpreted the Old Testament symbolically as a work of political science, and set out in an appendix Coleridge's theory of symbols; but the second descended more nearly to practical concerns, and was, as Coleridge forlornly insisted, 'meant to be *popular*'. *Zapolya*, *Biographia Literaria* and *Sibylline Leaves* all appeared in 1817. A lengthy *Treatise on Method* appeared as a prefatory chapter to the

Opposite page:

View over London, *by John Constable (1822), across open country and towards the city with the dome of St Paul's Cathedral visible. In his* Life of Sterling *Thomas Carlyle recalls Coleridge's view: 'Waving blooming country of the brightest green; dotted all over with handsome villas … and … under olive-tinted haze, the illimitable limitary ocean of London, with its domes and steeples definite in the sun, big Paul's, and the many memories attached to it hanging high over all'.*

The British Museum 1888–2–15–52

new *Encyclopaedia Metropolitana* in January 1818; and a third, much revised edition of *The Friend* in November. Coleridge's aptitude for business had not improved, and his dealings with publishers brought much anxiety and little income, so he returned to lecturing, delivering a course on European literature from the Middle Ages to the age of Queen Anne in the spring, and two series, one on the history of philosophy and one on Shakespeare, which began at the end of the year and went on into 1819. In the following years in Highgate he would publish *Aids to Reflection* (1825) and *On the Constitution of the Church and State* (1830), both works that would have an important influence on the development of Anglican theology. He placed articles in *Blackwood's Magazine*; and, in 1825 he lectured 'On the Prometheus of Æschylus' to the Royal Society of Literature, an extraordinary, extremely dense symbolical analysis of Greek myth, which took Coleridge an hour and twenty-five minutes to deliver and (as he ruefully conceded) left most of the audience bewildered. Substantial new editions of his poetical works appeared in 1828, 1829 and 1834. *Aids to Reflection and Church and State* went into second editions.

All the while, work advanced on the interminable, proliferating *Magnum Opus* or *Opus Maximum*, the summation of his philosophical life to which he considered all his other works supplementary. *Aids to Reflection*, not an insubstantial book, was but a 'little Pioneer' to the great work, 'in which my whole mind will be systematically unfolded' – 'my Opus Magnum on Revelation & Christianity, the Reservoir of my Reflections & Reading for 25 years past'. No such work ever did appear, despite its imminence being prominently announced in *Biographia* and elsewhere, which made it an irresistible joke for the satirists. Like the gap in Wordsworth's overall body of work where *The Recluse* should have been, the absent *Magnum Opus* looms over all later Coleridge – sometimes in an oddly empowering way, as it allowed the works he did write a kind of provisional quality, freeing them up to be merely precursors of the real, but unforthcoming, masterwork. At other times, though, a despairing sense of a central and abiding failure seems to have grown overwhelming, as Coleridge recorded in some late verses: 'Work without Hope draws nectar in a sieve, | And Hope without an object cannot live'.

Coleridge came to enjoy Highgate society, and he was soon a local figure, 'a great favorite with all the little boys and girls of the village', a contemporary

recorded, 'who used to rush up to him affectionately and hold merry talks with him'. He befriended his neighbour the comic actor Charles Mathews, who did a celebrated impersonation of Coleridge encountering a chemist's boy: "'Boy, did you never reflect upon the magnificence and beauty of the external universe?" *Boy*. "No, sir, never"'. At this time, Highgate was a village quite separate from London, surrounded by woods and close to Hampstead Heath, where John Constable would paint some of his greatest landscapes and cloudscapes. Constable thought the view unsurpassed in Europe, and Coleridge was similarly enthusiastic, taking guests to high ground and showing them a panorama that, he said, called to mind the pastoral scenery of Milton's 'L'Allegro'. It was while he was out on one of his walks, in April 1819, that he happened to meet John Keats, who described the encounter in a letter to his brother and sister-in-law:

> *I walked with him at his alderman-after-dinner pace for near two miles I suppose. In those two Miles he broached a thousand things – let me see if I can give you a list – Nightingales – Poetry – on Poetical Sensation – Metaphysics – Different genera and species of Dreams – Nightmare – a dream accompanied by a sense of touch – single and double touch – a dream related – First and second consciousness – the difference explained between will and Volition – so say metaphysicians from a want of smoking the second consciousness – Monsters – the Kraken – Mermaids – Southey believes in them – Southey's belief too much diluted – a Ghost story – Good morning – I heard his voice as he came towards me – I heard it as he moved away – I had heard it all the interval – if it may be called so.*

Coleridge's second son, Derwent, went up to St John's College, Cambridge, in 1820; he would later became an Anglican minister. Sara, his daughter, was brilliant, precociously publishing the translation of a Latin work of anthropology in 1822. (In 1829, she married her cousin, Henry Nelson, which pleased Coleridge.) Hartley, however, was an acute anxiety. He had been made a Fellow of Oriel College, Oxford, much to Coleridge's pride – 'whatever I am, my Hartley is Fellow of Oriel' – but in 1820 his probationary status was not confirmed, because of irregular habits and drunkenness. Coleridge entered into a protracted and painful correspondence with the college that became a study in displaced self-description – 'the little fellow never shewed any excitement at the *thing*, whatever it was, but afterwards, often when it had been removed, smiled or capered on the arm as at the *thought* of it'. But there was no chance of Hartley's restitution, and, after an aborted attempt at teaching at Ambleside, he became an itinerant figure about Keswick, charming and learned, often drunk for days. It was a sad misrealisation of the wandering life his father had wished for him in 'Frost at Midnight'.

In 1823, the Gillmans moved to 3, The Grove, Highgate, where Coleridge established a study-bedroom in the attic. 'His room looks upon a delicious prospect of wood and meadow, with coloured gardens under the window, like an embroidery to the mantle', wrote Leigh Hunt, 'Here he cultivates his flowers, and has a set of birds for his pensioners, who come to breakfast with him'. Here a talented group of

philosophically-minded young men came to Coleridge's Thursday evening 'conversazioni' – or '*One*versazioni', as Coleridge himself candidly called them, recognising his tendency to monologue. He was the most celebrated talker of his time, a contemporary legend, and he appears in many journals and diaries of the age, soliloquising for hours at the dinner table. Of all Coleridge's books it was *Table Talk*, posthumously assembled from records of the great man speaking made by his nephew Henry Nelson Coleridge, that did most to help establish his reputation in the nineteenth century. But the most vivid, disenchanted, account of Coleridge the talker, is that of the Scottish essayist Thomas Carlyle:

The Grove, Highgate, with Coleridge in the foreground. An engraving from Lucy E. Watson's Coleridge at Highgate *(1925).*

The British Library, 10825.e.25

Coleridge's spacious attic study-bedroom at the Grove. Coleridge moved here with the Gillmans in the autumn of 1823; from 1830, illness increasingly confined him to his room.

The British Library, 10825.e.25

The good man, he was now getting old, towards sixty perhaps; and gave you the idea of a life that had been full of sufferings; a life heavy-laden, half-vanquished, still swimming painfully in seas of manifold physical and other bewilderment. Brow and head were round, and of massive weight, but the face was flabby and irresolute. The deep eyes, of a light hazel, were as full of sorrow as of inspiration; confused pain looked mildly from them, as in a kind of mild astonishment. The whole figure and air, good and amiable otherwise, might be called flabby and irresolute; expressive of weakness under possibility of strength. He hung loosely on his limbs, with knees bent, and stooping attitude; in walking, he rather shuffled than decisively stept; and a lady once remarked, he never could fix which side of the garden-walk would suit him best, but continually shifted, in corkscrew fashion, and kept trying both. A heavy-laden, high-aspiring and surely much-suffering man. His voice, naturally soft and good, had contracted itself into a plaintive snuffle and sing song; he spoke as if preaching, – you would have said, preaching earnestly and also hopelessly the weightiest things. I still recollect his 'object' and 'subject,' terms of continual recurrence in the Kantean province; and how he sung and snuffled them into 'om-m-mject' and 'sum-m-mject,' with a kind of solemn shake or quaver, as he rolled along. No talk, in his century or in any other, could be more surprising.

Carlyle was pleased to find Coleridge's talk incomprehensible, and others, including Wordsworth, Byron and Hazlitt, came to lament Coleridge's absorption in metaphysics and theological abstraction. But others in Coleridge's wide and often brilliant circle found his monologue more illuminating, and his influence on nineteenth-century thought in England is immense. His writings, especially *Aids to Reflection*, were much esteemed in America too, and perhaps more highly. 'I am a poor poet in England', Coleridge told a young admirer, 'but I am a great philosopher in America'.

Coleridge regularly spent his holidays at Ramsgate, usually alone in the company of Mrs Gillman – something which occasioned gossip. He loved the

A view of Ramsgate by William Daniell. Coleridge loved the seaside and often spent his holidays at Ramsgate, in the company of Mrs Ann Gillman.

The British Library, 189.e.12

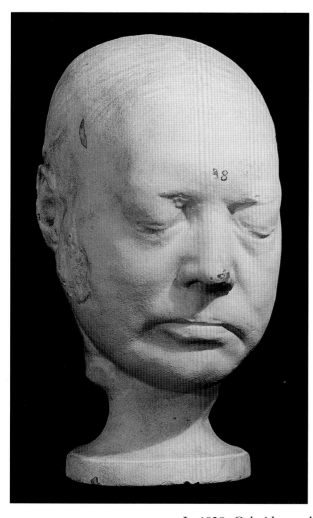

A life mask of Coleridge made in 1825 by the celebrated phrenologist J.G. Spurzheim. Coleridge was fond of Spurzheim but remained sceptical about the merits of phrenology (which sought to deduce personality traits from the shape of the head).

seaside, and was a keen sea-bather, enjoying 'a glorious tumble in the waves', and much appreciating the bathing machine, a contraption that you drove into the water from which to launch yourself – as he reported back to Gillman at Highgate: 'It was glorious! I watched each time from the top-step for a high Wave coming, and then with my utmost power of projection *shot* myself *off* into it, for all the world like a Congreve Rocket into a Whale.' During his 1823 holiday, the seaside jollity was disturbed by the news that Sara Hutchinson was also staying at the resort. Coleridge dined with her, and she was obviously friendly and pleased to see him. There is no certain hint of any profounder feelings in Coleridge, but perhaps his regrets about Sara stirred in the sad verses of self-lament he wrote about this time in the notebook – 'O youth! for years so many, so sweet | It seemed that Thou & I were one, | That still I nurse the fair deceit | And scarce believe that thou are gone!'.

In 1828, Coleridge undertook a more ambitious excursion – a tour through the Rhineland with Wordsworth and his daughter Dora. Relations were cordial again, if not intimate, and Coleridge's admiration for Wordsworth was unshaken. At a breakfast shortly before their trip, Crabb Robinson had called Coleridge 'Southey' by mistake, and his diary records Coleridge's response: '"Pray do not make such a blunder again. I should have no objection to your doing it with him." (Pointing to Wordsworth)'. Coleridge had judged Wordsworth 'the best poet of the age' in 1796, and in *Aids to Reflection* he was still named as 'the great Poet of our Age' – even though Coleridge now objected to the nature-worship of 'Tintern Abbey' and other Wordsworth poems with which he had once concurred. Coleridge could sound peculiarly vehement about the change in his religious views – as a professor found when he presumed that Coleridge meant much the same by the words 'Nature' and 'God'. 'I think God and Nature the same!' Coleridge replied indignantly, 'I think Nature is the devil in a strait-waistcoat!' God and nature had kept a very close association in the thought of the Unitarian Coleridge, but the older thinker was determined to keep them apart – God was no longer to be found through the sensory world of nature, but through the ideal world of the mind. 'The pith of my system', as Coleridge told his nephew, 'is to make the senses out of the mind – not the mind out of the senses'.

From 1830, Coleridge's health began to decline markedly, and in July of that year he told Poole he had 'been brought to the brink of the Grave'. His daughter and her husband settled in Hampstead, and Mrs Coleridge joined them, leaving Keswick after thirty years. The couple became friendly again, brought together as grandparents: 'the lack of Oil or Anti-friction Powder in our Conjugal Carriage-wheels did not extend to our parental relations', Coleridge announced to a friend after his daughter Sara's second child was baptised, adding, 'and in fact, bating living in the same house with her there are few women, that I have a greater respect & *ratherish* liking for, than Mrs C–'. 'His power of continuous talking seems unabated', Mrs Coleridge reported to Poole of the same occasion, 'for he talked incessantly for full 5 hours' – to 'the great entertainment' of the company, she added.

By the end of 1832 Coleridge was prematurely old and often in pain. He revived a little in 1833, when he attended the British Association meeting in Cambridge, and went to stay again in Ramsgate, but by the late spring of 1834 he was very ill. He died, in Highgate, on 25 July. On his deathbed he repeated 'his formula of the Trinity', mentally unimpaired to the end, as his daughter reported to Hartley: 'he remarked that his intellect was quite unclouded & he said "I could even be witty"'.

Speaking after Coleridge's death, Wordsworth called him 'the most wonderful man that he had ever known – wonderful for the originality of his mind, and the power he possessed of throwing out in profusion grand central truths' – 'wonderful' being the epithet which Dorothy had used on her first acquaintance with him almost forty years before. His great philosophical masterwork remained unfinished, and he was painfully aware of his contemporary reputation as 'the wild eccentric Genius

Samuel Taylor Coleridge

A portrait of the old Coleridge (1833) by Daniel Maclise, drawn to illustrate an article in Fraser's Magazine *in the series 'Gallery of Literary Characters'.*

Victoria and Albert Museum

that has published nothing but fragments & splendid Tirades'. But for modern readers, his achievement is less elusive: his collected works stretch to more than thirty volumes, besides his notebooks and his marvellous letters. He is author of some of the most famous poems in the language, and half of one of its most momentous poetic collaborations, a superbly suggestive and enlightening critic, and our most dazzling and assiduous theorist of the imagination. He was one of the most remarkable figures in one of the most remarkable periods of English literary history, and his influence on later writers and thinkers is immense. As a bereft Charles Lamb wrote: 'Never saw I his likeness, nor probably the world can see again'.

Chronology

1772   Samuel Taylor Coleridge born on 21 October at Ottery St Mary, Devon.

1778   Joins Ottery Grammar School.

1781   Death of Coleridge's father.

1782   Enters Christ's Hospital.

1788   Made a Grecian (top scholar) at Christ's Hospital.

1789   The fall of the Bastille in Paris.

1791   Enters Jesus College, Cambridge.

1792   Wins the Browne Medal for a Greek Ode on 'the Slave Trade'.

1793   Attends trial of William Frend; enlists in 15th Light Dragoons as Silas Tomkyn Comberbache.

1794   Returns to Cambridge; meets Robert Southey and plans Pantisocracy (June); engaged to Sara Fricker (August); *The Fall of Robespierre* (written with Southey) published (September); leaves Cambridge without degree, and stays in London with Charles Lamb (December); begins *Religious Musings* (Christmas Eve).

1795   Returns to Bristol; lectures published on politics and religion; Pantisocracy abandoned after Southey withdraws; first meeting with Wordsworth (September); marries Sara Fricker (4 October) and moves to Clevedon; writes 'The Eolian Harp' (August–October).

1796   Tours Midlands to publicise *The Watchman* (ten issues March–May); *Poems on Various Subjects* published (April); Hartley Coleridge born (September); moves to Nether Stowey, Somerset with family.

1797   Friendship with Worthworth develops; William and Dorothy Wordsworth, and Charles and Mary Lamb, stay at Stowey; Coleridge writes 'This Lime-Tree Bower My Prison'; Wordsworths move to Alfoxden, near Stowey; Coleridge publishes a second edition of *Poems*; writes 'Kubla Khan' and Part One of 'Christabel'; attempts at collaboration with Wordsworth fail and Coleridge begins 'The Ancient Mariner'; works for the *Morning Post*.

1798   Accepts Wedgwood annuity; Berkeley born (May); finishes 'The Ancient Mariner'; writes 'Frost at Midnight', 'France: An Ode', and 'Fears in Solitude' – published as a book later in the year; *Lyrical Ballads* (co-authored with Wordsworth) published, containing 'The Ancient Mariner'; travels to Germany with the Wordsworths and Wordsworth begins *The Prelude*, the 'Poem to Coleridge'.

1799   The Wordsworths return to England while Coleridge studies in Göttingen; Berkeley dies (February); Coleridge returns (July); visits the Lakes with Wordsworth (autumn), and falls in love with Sara Hutchinson; travels to London (November).

1800   Works as a successful journalist on the *Morning Post* (January-April); moves into Greta Hall, Keswick (July); Derwent born (September); Part Two of 'Christabel' written but not finished, and the poem is dropped from the next edition of *Lyrical Ballads*.

1801   Second edition of *Lyrical Ballads* ('1800') published under Wordsworth's name, with a new 'Preface', at least partly the fruit of Coleridge's thinking; Coleridge in London writing for the *Morning Post* (end of the year).

1802   Returns north hearing Sara Hutchinson is ill; writes 'Letter to Sara Hutchinson'; 'Dejection: An Ode' (a version of 'Letter') published in the *Morning Post* on his wedding anniversary (and Wordsworth's wedding day); Sara Coleridge born (23 December).

1803   Increasingly sick; publishes a third edition of *Poems*; begins a tour of Scotland with the Wordsworths.

1804   Travels to Malta (April); appointed secretary to Governor.

1805   John Wordsworth dies at sea.

1806   Visits Rome; returns to England and is back at Greta in October; decides to separate from Mrs Coleridge.

1807   Coleridge and Hartley at Coleorton with the Wordsworths; Wordsworth recites *The Prelude*, and Coleridge writes 'To William Wordsworth' in response; moves to London (November).

1808   Lodges at the *Courier* office; lectures at the Royal Institution on poetry; moves to Grasmere (September) and stays with the Wordsworths at Allan Bank.

1809   Publishes a periodical, *The Friend*, June 1809–March 1810, working with Sara Hutchinson.

1810   Travels to London with Basil Montagu, who passes on Wordsworth's disparaging remarks; lives with the Morgans in Hammersmith.

1811   Lectures (November 1811–January 1812) about Shakespeare and Milton.

1812   Last brief visit to the Lakes, returning to London in March; reissues *The Friend*, lectures on Shakespeare and Milton again (November 1812–January 1813).

1813   *Remorse* plays at the Drury Lane theatre (January); moves to Bristol following Morgan's bankruptcy and lectures on Shakespeare and Milton; taken seriously ill.

1814   Lectures in Bristol again; moves to Ashley, Wiltshire, and moves in with the Morgans in Calne (December).

1815   Dictates *Biographia Literaria* to Morgan, and prepares *Sibylline Leaves* for press.

1816   Accepted as house patient by Dr James Gillman at Highgate. 'Christabel', 'Kubla Khan' and 'The Pains of Sleep' published in a volume by John Murray. The first of three projected *Lay Sermons* published.

1817   The second *Lay Sermon*; *Biographia Literaria*, and *Sibylline Leaves* published.

1818   *Treatise on Method* published; further literary lectures; prepares a revised edition of *The Friend*; lectures on the history of philosophy, and gives his last series of lectures on literature (ending March 1819).

1819   Meets Keats in Millfield Lane, Highgate in April. Hartley Coleridge is elected a Fellow of Oriel College, Oxford.

1820   Hartley loses his Fellowship.

1825   Publishes *Aids to Reflection*, and lectures to the Royal Society of Literature 'On the Prometheus of Aeschylus'.

1828   Publishes his *Poetical Works* (3 vols.); a second edition follows in 1829; goes on a European tour with Wordsworth and Wordsworth's daughter Dora.

1830   Publishes *On the Constitution of the Church and State*.

1834   Coleridge dies, 25 July.

≈ *Further Reading*

The standard edition is *The Collected Works of Samuel Taylor Coleridge*, published in sixteen volumes (many in several parts) by Princeton University Press and Routledge, under the general editorship of Kathleen Coburn. I have drawn here especially upon the *Biographia Literaria*, ed. James Engell and W. Jackson Bate (2 vols., 1983), and the *Lectures 1808–1819 On Literature*, ed. R. A. Foakes (2 vols., 1987). The elaborate six-volume text of the poetical works prepared by J. C. C. Mays for the *Collected Works* is a remarkable achievement, but most readers may find the Everyman edition edited by John Beer (revised edition, 1999), or William Keach's Penguin edition (1997), more readily useable. I have also quoted from *The Collected Letters of Samuel Taylor Coleridge*, ed. Earl Leslie Griggs (6 vols., Oxford University Press, 1956–71), and *The Notebooks of Samuel Taylor Coleridge*, ed. Kathleen Coburn, Merton Christensen, and Anthony John Harding (5 vols., each in two parts, Princeton University Press, *etc.*, 1957–2002).

Letters by the Wordsworths are taken from *The Letters of William and Dorothy Wordsworth: The Early Years, 1787–1805*, ed. Ernest de Selincourt, rev. Chester L. Shaver (Clarendon Press, 1967) and *The Letters of William and Dorothy Wordsworth: The Middle Years*, ed. Ernest de Selincourt, rev. Mary Moorman and Alan G. Hill (2 vols., Clarendon Press, 1969–70). Dorothy Wordsworth's journals have been quoted from the edition of the *Grasmere Journals* by Pamela Woof (Clarendon Press, 1991). Dorothy's account of the tour of Scotland is available in the old edition of her journals by de Selincourt (2 vols., Macmillan, 1941).

Sara Coleridge's letters to Thomas Poole are collected in *Minnow Among Tritons*, ed. Stephen Potter (Nonesuch Press, 1934). I have also drawn on the early, unfinished biography of Coleridge by his friend and physician James Gillman – *The Life of Samuel Taylor Coleridge* (only one vol. published, Pickering, 1838) – for which Coleridge himself was a prime source. Other contemporary records are drawn from *Samuel Taylor Coleridge: Interviews and Recollections*, ed. Seamus Perry (Palgrave, 2000).

Three contemporaries offer good places to begin exploring: Charles Lamb's 'Christ's Hospital Five and Thirty Years Ago', in Lamb's *Essays of Elia* (1823); William

Hazlitt's 'Mr. Coleridge', in his *The Spirit of the Age* (1825), and 'My First Acquaintance with Poets', first published in *The Liberal* (1823), and often collected; and Thomas De Quincey's 'Samuel Taylor Coleridge', first published in *Tait's Magazine* (1834–1835) and conveniently available in *Recollections of the Lakes and Lake Poets*, ed. David Wright (Penguin, 1970, often reprinted). There are charismatic and suggestive essays by Leslie Stephen ('Coleridge', in *Hours in a Library*, 1879), E. M. Forster ('Silas Tomkyn Comberbache', in *Abinger Harvest*, 1934) and Virginia Woolf ('Coleridge', in *The Death of the Moth*, 1942).

The following works might be especially recommended to readers new to Coleridge: Rosemary Ashton, *The Life of Samuel Taylor Coleridge: A Critical Biography* (Blackwell, 1996); Walter Jackson Bate, *Coleridge* (Macmillan, 1969); John Beer, *Coleridge the Visionary* (Chatto and Windus, 1959); Kathleen Coburn, *The Self Conscious Imagination* (Oxford University Press, 1974); Richard Holmes, *Coleridge: Early Visions* (Hodder and Stoughton, 1989) and *Coleridge: Darker Reflections* (HarperCollins, 1998); Humphry House, *Coleridge* (Rupert Hart-Davis, 1953); Molly Lefebure, *The Bondage of Love: A Life of Mrs Samuel Taylor Coleridge* (Gollancz, 1986); Thomas McFarland, *Romanticism and the Forms of Ruin* (Princeton University Press, 1980); and Nicholas Roe, *Wordsworth and Coleridge: The Radical Years* (Clarendon Press, 1988). Kathleen Coburn's anthology *Inquiring Spirit: A New Presentation of Coleridge from his Published and Unpublished Prose Writings* (Routledge and Kegan Paul, 1951) is an attractive introduction to the wide range of the prose, made by Coleridge's most devoted modern student. John Spencer Hill's anthology *Imagination in Coleridge* (Macmillan, 1978) is helpful and well-annotated. John Beer is general editor of a useful series of thematically organised series, *Coleridge's Writings*, published by Macmillan/Palgrave (1990–).

⁓ *Index*

Adams, Joseph 107, 109
Alfoxden Park 40–1
Allan Bank 90–1
Allston, Washington 84, 102

Ball, Alexander 79–81, 95
Balliol College, Oxford 17
Beaumont, George 71, 75, 85, 86
Berkeley, George 39
Bertozzi, Cecilia 81, 83
Bowdon (uncle) 10
Bowles, William Lisle 13–14, 105
Bowyer (or Boyer), James 12
Brent, Charlotte 89
Bristol 19, 26, 36, 89
Butler, Samuel 14
Byron, George Gordon 107, 108, 117

Calne 102
Carlyon, Clement 55, 56
Chester, John 52, 54
Coleorton 86–7
Coleridge, Ann (née Bowdon; mother) 7, 8, 10
Coleridge, Anne (sister) 8
Coleridge, Berkeley (son) 52, 54
Coleridge, David Hartley (son) 34, 56, 62, 87, 96, 102, 114
Coleridge, Derwent (son) 62, 96, 114
Coleridge, Francis (brother) 8, 9–10
Coleridge, George (brother) 8, 14, 15, 16, 23, 25
Coleridge, Henry Nelson (son-in-law) 114, 119
Coleridge, James (brother) 8, 97
Coleridge, John (father) 7–8, 9, 10
Coleridge, Luke (brother) 8
COLERIDGE, Samuel Taylor
 appearance 23, 28, 55;
 birthday, his lifelong mistake about date of 7;
 childhood favourite 8;
 deathbed 119;
 depression, loneliness and dejection 8, 37, 82–3, 86, 96, 112;
 dragoon, enlists in 16;
 dreaminess 8–9;
 drinking 14, 55, 98;
 French revolution, impact of 12–13, 15, 27;
 great philosophical work, ambitions and plans for 55, 71, 102–3, 112, 119–20;
 Jesus College, Cambridge, studies at 14–16, 23;
 journalism 31–3, 58–9, 65, 68, 97;
 illnesses 64, 65, 75, 96, 102, 107, 119; *and see* opium;
 lectures: on Belles Lettres 101; on politics and religion 26–8; on European literature 112; on fine arts 85; on literature 89–90, 98–101;
 love for Sara Hutchinson 57, 66, 73, 87, 95, 97;
 marriage 23, 26, 29, 54–5, 66, 68, 85, 86, 119; *and see* Coleridge, Sara;
 name, his discontent with his 8;
 nightmares 75;
 opium, taking of 43, 64, 66, 73, 96, 107, 110;
 Pantisocracy 19, 22–3, 24, 28, 31, 34;
 poet, himself no 62;

poetry and the imagination, ideas of 14, 30–1, 37, 43–4, 68, 81–2, 89–90, 104–6; *and see* Shakespeare, criticism of;
portrayed: by Gillray 24; by Hazlitt 26; by Dorothy Wordsworth 38; by a drunk Dane 54; by De Quincey 88; by Carlyle 116–17;
radicalism 7, 12–13, 14–15, 17–18, 23, 24, 26–7, 28, 31; *and see* Pantisocracy;
reciting poetry 47, 107;
religious opinions 17, 25–6, 38–9, 40, 45, 54–5, 56, 106, 118–19; *and see* Unitarianism;
schooling: grammar school 9, 10; Christ's Hospital 10–14;
Shakespeare, his criticism of 89–90, 98–101;
Silas Tomkyn Comerbache, assumes name of 16;
spied upon 42;
talking: 38, 47, 55, 84, 88, 97, 107, 115; preaching Pantisocracy 19; preaching in chapel 25–6; *and see* lecturing;
Unitarianism of 15, 24–5, 28, 30, 47; his rejection of 82, 118–19;
walking: in the Hartz mountains 55; from Keswick to Grasmere 61, 67; in the Lakes 56–7, 61–2, 69–70, 95; in the Quantocks 19, 38, 41, 49; to Racedown 37–8; in Scotland 71, 73; in Wales 17, 19, 70;
Wordsworth, Dorothy, admiration for 38;
Wordsworth, William, admiration for 36–7, 38, 41, 51–2, 59, 63, 83, 86–7, 105, 118; collaboration with 45, 52; criticism of 73, 106–7; despair and bitterness at perceived rejection by 96, 97–8; sense of literary difference from 63, 68–9, 106–7; scheme for *The Recluse* and 51–2, 56, 83; separating from the Wordsworths in Scotland 71–3
WORKS: POETRY:
'Ancient Mariner, The' 45–7, 52, 60, 63, 83;
Brook, The (unwritten) 51–2;
'Christabel' 49–50, 62, 108;
Christabel (volume) 108;
'Dejection: An Ode' 8, 44, 67, 71, 106;
'Eolian Harp, The' 30, 33, 56, 66;
Fall of Robespierre, The (co-authored) 19;
'Fears in Solitude' 51, 53;
Fears in Solitude (volume) 52–3;
'France: An Ode' 51, 52–3;
'Frost at Midnight' 10, 31, 50–1, 53;
'Kubla Khan' 43–4, 75, 107;
'Letter to Sara Hutchinson' 10, 66–7;
'Lines written at Shurton Bars' 30;
Lyrical Ballads 52; second edition 60, 61, 62–3;
Mahomet (co-authored) 56;
'Nightingale, The' 31, 51;
Osorio 34, 101;
'Pains of Sleep, The' 75, 108, 110;
Poems, on Various Subjects 33–4;
Poems (second edition) 34–5; *Poems* (third edition) 71;
'Reflections on having Left a Place of Retirement' 31;
'Religious Musings' 24–5, 33, 37, 56;
Sibylline Leaves 103;
'This Lime-Tree Bower my Prison' 30, 38–9, 46;
'To a Young Ass' 24, 33;

'To Fortune' 16;
'To William Wordsworth' 87;
'Wanderings of Cain, The' 45;
'Work without Hope' 112;
Zapolya 103, 111
PROSE:
  Aids to Reflection 112, 117;
  'Answer to Godwin' (unwritten) 37;
  Biographia Literaria 12, 13–14, 42, 44, 68–9, 103–7, 111;
  Conciones ad Populum 31;
  Friend, The 12–13, 91, 94–5, 101, 112;
  Lay Sermons 110–11;
  Lessing, Gotthold, study of (unwritten) 60;
  Notebooks 51, 57, 59, 61, 73, 78, 81–2, 90, 118;
  Omniana (co–authored) 101;
  On the Constitution of the Church and State 112;
  Schiller, Friedrich, translations of 59–60;
  Seven Lectures on Shakespeare and Milton 98;
  Table Talk 115;
  Treatise on Method 111–12;
  'Upholder, The' (later *The Friend*) 91;
  Watchman, The 31–3
Coleridge, Sara (Sarah, née Fricker; wife) 22–3, 26, 29–30, 38, 54–5, 58, 59, 65, 68, 69–70, 71, 73, 85, 86–7, 89, 95–6, 119
Coleridge, Sara (daughter) 70–1, 91, 114, 119
Collier, John Payne 98
Constable, John 113
Cottle, Joseph 33–4, 88

Davy, Humphry 65, 91
De Quincey, Thomas 88, 89, 90
Dove Cottage, Grasmere 59

Evans, Mary 12, 23
Evans, Tom 12

Farington, Joseph 90
Frend, William 15
Fricker, Edith 22
Fricker, Mary 22
Fricker, Sara: *see* Coleridge, Sara

Gillman, Ann 110, 117–18
Gillman, James 12, 64, 109, 110, 118
Gillray, James 24
Godwin, William 17, 28, 37, 59, 71
Goslar 54
Göttingen 55
Greta Hall, Keswick 60, 65, 75, 95

Hamburg 54
Hartley, David 34
Hazlitt, William 26, 41, 47, 117
Highgate 109, 112–13
Hucks, Joseph 17, 19
Hunt, Leigh 12, 107, 114
Hutchinson, Joanna 56
Hutchinson, Mary: *see* Wordsworth, Mary
Hutchinson, Sara 56, 57–8, 66, 86–7, 91, 94–5, 118
Hutchinson, Tom 56

Kant, Immanuel 105
Keats, John 113–14
Klopstock, Friedrich 54

Lamb, Charles 11, 23–4, 26, 30, 34–5, 38, 40, 59, 98, 101, 107, 110, 121
Lamb, Mary 38
Lloyd, Charles 35
London 58, 65, 96, 97
Lovell, Robert 19, 22

Malta 75, 78–83
Mathews, Charles 113
Mitford, Mary Russell 98
Montagu, Basil 96
Morgan, John 89, 97, 98, 102, 107, 108
Morgan, Mary 89, 97, 98, 102

Nether Stowey 34, 38
Northcote, James 75

Oriel College, Oxford 114

Pinney brothers 36
Poole, John 22
Poole, Thomas 17, 19–20, 30, 34, 54, 60, 65, 73, 75, 88, 95, 96, 119
Priestley, Joseph 25, 28

Racedown, Dorset 37–8
Ramsgate 117–18
Ratzeburg 54
Robinson, Henry Crabb 90, 97, 98, 100, 101, 110
Rogers, Samuel 98
Rome 84

Salutation and Cat 23–4, 26
Shelvocke, George 45
Sheridan, Richard Brinsley 43
Sockburn-on-Tees 56, 57
Southey, Robert 17, 19, 23, 26, 28–9, 38, 52, 56, 73, 85, 86–7, 95
Spinoza, Baruch 42, 56
'Spy Nozy' 42–3
Staël, Anna Louise Germaine de 97
Stuart, Daniel 57, 85–6
Syracuse 81, 83

Thelwall, John 34, 41–3, 63, 65
Tieck, Ludwig 84

Wade, Josiah 102
Watchet 45
Wedgwood, Josiah 47, 52, 55
Wedgwood, Tom 47, 52, 55, 70
Wordsworth, Dora 118
Wordsworth, Dorothy 37–8, 40, 54, 56, 57, 62, 65, 67, 71–3, 75, 78, 86–7, 91, 95, 98, 119
Wordsworth, John 57, 82
Wordsworth, Mary 56, 67
Wordsworth, William 17, 31, 36– 8, 40–1, 42, 45, 47, 48, 51–2, 54, 56–7, 60, 62, 63, 65, 67, 71–3, 75, 85, 86–7, 90, 91–2, 95–6, 97, 98, 101, 110, 117 118, 119
  WORKS: *The Prelude* (the 'Poem to Coleridge') 54, 57, 78, 87; *The Recluse* 53–4, 75, 86, 95, 112; *see also Lyrical Ballads* (under Coleridge: WORKS: POETRY)

Acknowledgements

This book was completed during a period of study leave from the University of Glasgow, funded by the Arts and Humanities Research Board; and I thank both institutions for their generosity. I should also thank my patient editors at the British Library, Lara Speicher and Charlotte Lochhead. I am especially indebted to Nicola Trott for much encouragement and help.

The British Library is grateful to the following for permission to reproduce illustrations: Bridgeman Art Library, Bristol Central Library, The British Museum, Exeter Museums and Art Gallery, Jesus College, Cambridge, Leeds City Art Gallery, Leicester City Museums, Maidstone Museum and Art Gallery, the National Archives, National Gallery of Scotland, National Maritime Museum, National Portrait Gallery (London), Tate Gallery, Trustees of Keswick School, Victoria and Albert Museum, Whitworth Art Gallery, Manchester, William Ramsey Henderson Trust and the Wordsworth Trust. While every effort has been made to trace and acknowledge all copyright holders, we would like to apologise for any errors or omissions.

Front cover illustrations: *St Mary Redcliffe* by John Sell Cotman (The British Library 1859–5–28–117); Part of a manuscript of 'Kubla Khan' (The British Library, Add. MS 50847 recto); *Samuel Taylor Coleridge* by George Dance 1804 (The Wordsworth Trust)

Back cover illustration: *Samuel Taylor Coleridge* by Washington Allston (National Portrait Gallery)

Half title page: *Samuel Taylor Coleridge* by Peter Vandyke (National Portrait Gallery)

Frontispiece: Part of a manuscript copy of 'Kubla Khan' (The British Library, Add. MS 50847 f.60)

Contents page: *Keswick Lake and Skiddaw* by Francis Towne (Leeds City Art Gallery)

First published in 2003 by The British Library, 96 Euston Road, London NW1 2DB

Text © Seamus Perry 2003

Illustrations © The British Library 2003 and other named copyright holders

British Library Cataloguing in Publication Data
A catalogue for this title is available from The British Library

ISBN 0 7123 4787 9

Designed and typeset by Crayon Design, Stoke Row, Henley-on-Thames
Map by John Mitchell
Colour and black-and-white origination by South Sea International Press
Printed in Hong Kong by South Sea International Press